Blackbird I

Blackbird Flying
The Story of a Stroke Survivor

Cate Collinson

YouCaxton Publications
Oxford & Shrewsbury

YouCaxton Publications
enquiries@youcaxton.co.uk

To my lovely son Jason.

Special thanks are due to:

Julia Dohnal: Special thanks for the many times you spent with me offering positivity and encouragement and support.
Again, thank you very much indeed.

Stephen: My helpmate and very much my partner, and reading through the book.

Debi: Lots of chatting and coffee in Chichester, and beneficial about my book.

Chris - Now sadly passed away but always remembered.

Extra special thanks to my editor Alison Williams

'Don't be disabled in spirit as well as physically,'
Professor Stephen Hawking

Contents

Preface

This is Emma's story, in her own words; ninety-five percent of it is true.

Mark and Emma meet in 1983, when Mark gives her a lift from Holland to England, leaving her husband and son in Dordrecht. After three months of friendship, they fall in love. Mark goes to work in Saudi Arabia, and he helps Emma to buy a house in Crystal Palace Lane, West Dulwich, returning to England every four months.

The relationship is not a happy one, however. Mark is prone to drink and after he comes back to England, he is drinking almost every day. Emma, suffering from guilt about so many things, stressing out from overwork, running, cycling, smoking and drinking too much, has a devastating stroke which leaves her with problems down her right-hand side and great difficulties in speaking.

After a few months of recovery, she is moved to a specialist stroke unit, but is aghast to find that all of her fellow patients are much older. Emma convinces Mark to let her come home and she arranges physiotherapy and eventually a course of speech therapy.

Mark moves upstairs in the same house and carries on his virtually single life.

Slowly Emma gets her life back together again, with the help of friends and hobbies such as singing and pottery, and particularly riding her bike. Ten years after her stroke and following three months training, she completes the Stroke Association Bike Ride, crossing twenty-four bridges from Tower Hill to Hampton Court. A year later she rides from

Croydon to Brighton with colleagues from a stroke support group, Different Strokes.

This story is not only for stroke survivors, but for anyone who has had a trauma in their lives, or who might be interested in her narrative.

A blackbird is a repeating and comforting motif in the story.

Chapter 1:

Catastrophe

April 23rd, 1986

I get off the bus at the top of Regent Street, at the corner of Oxford Street. I take my time crossing over, and I smile and look up to the clear blue sky; I can see it's a beautiful day, even so early.

I close my eyes for a second, and I don't know that in less than three hours, my life will change completely. It will be a catastrophe for me, and anybody who is close to me.

I carry on to the right to Oxford Street and to Tottenham Court Road, and I turn left, to where, in the huge building on my left, is my temporary office.

I arrive at dead on nine o'clock, and work solidly until just after eleven, when I go to the coffee machine and get a drink, and I have a smoke as well, the first cigarette of the day. I swallow two paracetamol with the coffee, to send the headache away. I've had a dull stabbing pain for at least a fortnight, and I feel more and more sick every day. I make a mental note; I must go to the doctors.

***

I go to the toilet, and as I'm peeing, I start to feel very strange. I realise that my right side is numb! I'm looking at my arm, not knowing what's going on, and gradually I'm leaning over on my right side, now falling, very, very slowly, slipping, slipping, and I can't hold on to anything with my right hand.

Then I'm on the floor that feels cold even though it is warm in the building. I can't call out; something's stopping me.

Although there's calmness within me as I lie on the ground, looking at the ceiling.

After a minute or so, a girl comes in – she can see my leg sticking out from under the door. She is calling to me, as she tries to get the door open. The girl is saying something, but I can't make head nor tail of it. Then, she's dashing out to get some help, and someone rings 999.

Sometime after, the girl and two of her colleagues come in, and one of the girls is trying to get the door open again, but she can't. She's almost shouting something; I can see her underneath the toilet door, as she bends down, observing me with some empathy.

When the paramedics arrive, they ask the girl who found me who I am. "We don't know, she only arrived yesterday afternoon, sorry."

She looks as though she isn't coping with this, with me lying on the ground. It's too much for her, and she quickly leaves, along with her two colleagues.

Another girl comes in. "What's happening? I was at a meeting." She stares at me, shocked and surprised. "Will she be alright?"

The ambulance man is still looking at me, concern written all over his face. "I don't know! The person who rang the hospital said she fainted, that's all. Do you know what her name is?"

"Emma."

I know the voice. I stare at her with a funny blurry brain, and I can't place her. Also, I want to go to sleep, desperately.

The ambulance man is shouting at me as well. "Emma, can you hear me?" He seems to be far off, but at the same time I can see he's yelling.

"But I must to go to sleep though." I'm closing my eyes.

Now he's almost screaming at me. "Emma, Emma, can you hear me?"

"Yes, I can hear you." I am trying to speak, attempting to open my eyes again. I can't think, what's happening to me?

I desperately need to say the words coming out of my head, though I must also go to sleep.

After a minute, the ambulance man makes a final decision. "OK. She's not responding, let's get her on to the stretcher, and into the hospital as quickly as possible."

They put me on a stretcher, and we set off to the hospital, with the sirens blaring. By this time, I'm unconscious. Two hours later, after many tests, the doctors decide it's a stroke, even though I'm not old, I'm only thirty-nine. How can that be?

***

Doctor Rutherford has been away to Barbados for three weeks with his wife and two children; this is his first day back. He is staring at Mark, unsmiling and grim.

"Please, sit down, Mr. Hurst," he says, pointing to a bench behind them. "I'm sorry to tell you this, but we think it's a stroke. However, we won't know how bad it is until Emma wakes up." He is trying to be as gentle as possible.

There is a silence between them. Doctor Rutherford continues hesitantly. "It's always very difficult at these times, and I wish I could say more."

Mark is growing white. "The person I spoke to said my girlfriend had fainted, that's all. Now you're saying that she's had a stroke?"

Mark is agitated and nervous; he stands up and the doctor stands with him. "I kissed her goodbye at eight this morning and she was absolutely fine."

He desperately wants answers, and he is still glaring hard at the doctor.

"You can have a stroke at any minute, old and young. Tell me, has she been having any headaches or nausea, Mr. Hurst?"

Mark drops back down on the chair and nods his head. He puts his hands over his face then rubs them together as if they're cold, and he stares into nothing again, as he tries to take in more facts.

3

Finally he clears his throat. "Yes. She's been having headaches and nausea for a month, she was going to go to the doctor, but she didn't go, did she?" Mark shakes his head, looking at the doctor. "I should have made her... I didn't." He falls silent, burying his head in his hands.

"Can I see her now?"

"Of course, but be prepared for a little shock. Come this way."

Mark is still shaking as he looks at the figure on the hospital bed in the centre of the room. He walks towards the bed, the doctor closely following him.

Mark is trying to convince himself that it is a nightmare and in a minute he will wake up. Mentally, he is pinching himself, but this is not a dreadful dream, it is completely, utterly real. He stops; he is cold all over as he stares at the figure.

There are wires on my forehead, chest and arms. I look so peaceful, and I'm stirring, knowing that Mark is there in the room with me.

Mark leaves the room, in deep shock. He sits down before he falls down.

He can't get his head around it; only yesterday he met Emma in the pub after work, and he thought she looked great. What happened today?

**

Mark stops at Herne Hill station – the train has been shaking along as much as he has. He needs a drink.

In the pub he sees his friend Barry sitting at the bar, and he joins him, sinking two pints of Stella in quick succession.

"You alright?" asks Barry. He can see the tears in Mark's eyes.

Mark is gazing somewhere in space, but he answers Barry. "Emma has had a stroke. I can't believe it. We have to wait until she wakes up. That's the awful part. She was alright this morning... I can't believe it."

"I don't know what to say. She's a lovely girl, as well. You must be gutted." Barry stares at his beer.

Mark laughs, deep in his guts. "That's alright. What can anybody say?"

There is silence between them, and Mark can still see the figure on the bed, in that hospital room.

Eventually Barry softly says, "I can give you a lift home, if you want; I'm going in your direction. Do you want somebody with you?"

"No. That's alright, thank you. But do you mind, just one more pint."

Chapter 2:

Before

From the top of the railway bridge just before Dagley Lane in Shalford, a cow in a field by herself was yelling for her calf; it was an awful sound. I can still hear it today. But the bull calf was already dead or kept somewhere in the dark, because some people like veal.

At the end of the way, there was a wire fence on the left. My mother and I would crawl through into a field and I'd run down with our six dogs, into a long grassy valley with wild flowers - daisies, buttercups and king cups, cornflower, teasel and many, many more, until we reached the river, my mother following not far behind.

The Alsatian, Lona, dived into the river after my mother or I had thrown a stick into the water. She'd go and fetch it, time after time, and we'd get soaked on every occasion when she came out and shook herself, getting water all over us, us laughing as she did.

My mother did not hug and kiss me, but then I can still hear us laughing, the two of us; it was quite magical. I had forgotten the cow.

***

I met Matt when I was seventeen, he was two years old than me. I was living with my mother, grandmother, one Alsatian and five whippets in Arundel, a beautiful town with a 1000-year-old castle.

My parents were separated. My father went to live in Cranleigh, Surrey and he came to see me every fortnight.

Matt was short and stocky, because he had Perthes disease in his hip bone; apparently there was nothing his parents could have done about it when he was a child, subsequently, he had a slight limp. Matt had dark brown hair and blue eyes; he was a cheeky and mischievous musician.

Matt made me laugh and my mother chuckled at his sense of humour, and, as a result, my mother let me get on with life with him. She had dogs to look after, and she was a pet shop owner, besides, she clipped poodles.

My father was not so easily impressed with Matt, however Matt was somebody I got close to. Though my father voiced his opinion, in no uncertain terms either, and he restrained himself as much as possible, which was very difficult for him; he had quite a bad temper, I know, I was at the end of his exasperations sometimes when I was growing up.

Nonetheless, he said, "If you stay away from Matt for a month, and you feel the same way as you feel now, I won't stand in your way."

My father thought I was too young to attach myself to any one person, particularly when I was at college. At the same time, he didn't have any ambitions for me at all. But I did!

My sweet Great Auntie Collie made my dresses by hand when I was a child, and she gave me some money in her will, when she passed away. Previously she had gone to Canada where she'd met and married a Canadian. She came back with a Canadian accent when her husband passed away, which I thought was wonderful.

I thought, what shall I do with the money? I decided to go to college. I liked cooking, so I did a two-year hotel and catering course at a college in Chichester.

***

In November 1967, it was my twenty-first birthday - I got married a week later. Just before we went into the church, my father tried again to make me see sense. He was quite right, he still thought I was too young, and he didn't like Matt at all.

But Matt was like my father in various ways, and he stifled and supressed me, except I liked that. I was so young, that until I got away from him(which was much later), I didn't realise the consequences of that.

My father was damaged from the 2nd World War, bless him. Matt thought that's what you did with a wife - keep the reins on tightly.

So, my dad and I went around and round the Arundel square in the bridal car and my father stared at me and kept asking, "Are you sure you want to get married? Do you know what you're doing?" My father wasn't annoyed; however, he was very, very uneasy to say the least, but he didn't show it.

I didn't look at him, I didn't know what I wanted, I just nodded my head. I thought about a fun day out, I didn't think about tomorrow. Finally, my father gave up, and he breathed out and shook his head, but he took me to the church on time.

So, I dragged my father up the aisle, and, instead of slow and graceful, I almost sprinted, turning and thinking, 'Come on, come on,' to my two cousins, who I did not like. They were giggling behind me, and I could hear my aunt's tittering echoes behind me in the church.

My mother sat in the left-hand aisle; she was wearing a beautiful green dress, which shimmered with the light from the windows in the church. She'd had it made for the occasion, and a hat to match, and she looked better than I did, I thought. Clearly, I wasn't the only one to be seen that day, but maybe she was doing it for my father.

I joined Matt and we smiled nervously and giggled at each other, then we turned and faced the vicar, the Reverent Ravenscroft, who was nodding and smiling; he almost looked lovingly at us, his hands together in a prayer. Then his hands were parted, the right hand slowly and gently pointed down, and, without any words, we knelt down.

Then the vicar said loudly, "You have noticed the scaffolding, it's to do with the roof." His right hand pointed towards the gable, even beyond! "Please, please, give your change generously." He smiled and then we said our vows.

The reception was in a pub off Tarrant Street. A great time was had by all! I particularly fancied the best man.

***

Eighteen months later, Tom came along. Tom was a beautiful blond baby, and Matt was at the birth. Matt held him first, but only for a minute, as Tom had to go into an incubator, because he was only five pounds and two ounces. Tom was so tiny, I was in disbelief; he was so exquisite, and I had made him (and Matt of, course!).

The first time our baby laughed, he was in my arms, his head over my shoulder staring at the wonders of the world when something tickled him, and laughter came from somewhere deep in his tummy. That surprised him more, so he laughed more and more, and my mother, who was with us, and I laughed with him. It's a lovely memory.

While Tom was a baby, Matt carried on just as normal, going out, leaving me holding the baby and with no money to speak of, and I wasn't working full-time, only in dribs and drabs.

But I didn't know what time of day it was, I was naïve and guileless; as a result, I left for the first time in 1971 when Tom was eighteen months old. I had a job with the Ministry of Agriculture in Guildford as a punch card operator, not cooking or managing. I was bored, though it was a job. Tom went to a nursery and the first time I left him, I could hear him sobbing; however, he soon got used to it.

Then I moved to Brighton, via Arundel, where I used to live with my mother. I spent three months there, and, in due course, I found a place to rent in Hove, and put Tom with a child minder.

I was contracted into a catering agency in Hove. I was a manager or cook, for banks, schools, factories, covering the whole of Sussex; it was definitely varied, and I liked it very much, until the catering agency closed.

Soon after, Matt persuaded me to go back with him, but with no stipulations or conditions. I stupidly agreed.

I thought it was better for Tom to have a father. I didn't think about me at all.

I went back to Worthing where he was living. I had a gut feeling before I reached Worthing that I shouldn't be going back to Matt, but I went all the same. Eventually, we moved back to Brighton, and we had seven years there until Holland came into our lives. Matt was working in Dordrecht, Holland. I was working at a lovely vegetarian restaurant close by me, in Hove.

But then Matt said I could join him in Dordrecht. Matt told me that Tom, who was now nine, would have a good education there.

So, the restaurant went out of the window and I dutifully went to Dordrecht, Holland, taking Tom with me.

Chapter 3:

Holland

I had given up my work in the vegetarian restaurant the week before, and Tom would have gone back to school, instead we were leaving to go to Holland. I had a feeling, a gut feeling. 'Am I doing the right thing?'

I was doing the ironing, packing, getting everything ready to go. I gazed at Tom; he was reading his comic, it was an adventure for him, and he was going to see his dad. I know it was an adventure for me, but I was still very anxious. I went over and over it, but I knew I was going, and something drew me there, and we were soon carried over the seas to Rotterdam.

***

Matt was waiting for us in Rotterdam Central Station, leaning on a black van. He was wearing sunglasses and I couldn't see his eyes; my heart sank! Matt kissed, hugged and patted Tom on the head, and he kissed me quickly. We both smiled, and I hid my anguish until a little later. I got the feeling there was something worrying him.

We climbed into the van, leaving Rotterdam, and drove to Dordrecht, the oldest town in Holland with narrow streets and typically Dutch; some of the houses were built over the canals, there were bars on every street. Dordrecht seemed really lovely.

Then Matt dropped the bombshell - there was nowhere for Tom and I to stay in Dordrecht! We were going to a farm in a small village near the German border, called Dinxperlo, almost a hundred miles away.

I was furious with myself and Matt. I almost turned around with Tom, but I had nowhere to go.

I looked at Tom. 'What have I done?' I thought.

***

The more northeast we got, the colder it got; it was autumn. We were met by Francis Visser whose mother was English, but she had been brought up mainly in Holland. She was quite tall, precise and efficient. Kas Visser, who was Dutch, was very tall and plodding, with a long, long ginger goatee beard.

A week later, Tom started at a Dutch school. The first day he was nervous, naturally, but he managed to settle down in due course. We got on with life around the farm, and school, until Matt picked us up.

There was a beautiful big black horse, which I could ride when Tom was at school. There were goats at the farm, and we had milk, but we didn't like goats' milk much. However, we loved chickens, they were our feathered friends but they were frenzied when we tried tenderly to tip them off their nests to get the eggs.

Matt had some engagements around Holland, and then, finally, we went back to Dordrecht where we stayed for four and a half years.

Tom had a good experience in Holland in many ways; he learnt Dutch quickly and had an all-encompassing and excellent education, better than an English one, at Princess Juliana School. He liked it there and he worked hard; his Dutch was so good after six months his teacher thought he was Dutch, except, that is, for his English name, and he made some good friends there too.

After a while, we were given a council flat outside Dordrecht. It had two bedrooms, a kitchen, shower, and a medium-sized sitting room with a dining room combined; it was more than acceptable.

By now, we also had a dog called Buddy and a cat called Elvis; they were good friends. I took Buddy with me on bike rides beside the river nearby for miles; even Elvis would come for a little distance, but he always turned back home.

Matt was in a band, and I joined a choir with Frank Muir, Matt's saxophonist.

After ten rehearsals I was put at the centre of the choir. I had the highest voice, soprano. Tom turned up to our concerts, and my friends as well, but Matt did not.

***

I did various work, quite diverse, from office work to a factory, but again, no cooking. I could speak Dutch, going to shops and the market place, and I knew what they were saying in Dutch, but I couldn't talk back, also, they loved to talk in English, their second language.

We travelled a bit, once to Almeria in Spain, and I worked picking grapes in Switzerland.

However, I was homesick. I missed England after four and a half years in Holland, so we decided I would go to England first, and Matt and Tom, who was thirteen now, would follow me later.

Chapter 4:

Home Coming

Mark was a friend of Matt's; he was working in London and he gave me a lift from Holland. I had met him only twice briefly, with his wife, Di, once at their house with Matt, the other time was outside our flat, where Mark was helping to fix Matt's car.

Mark picked me up in Dordrecht and we drove to Bruges in Belgium, and waited to board the ferry to Dover which would take about four hours. On board, Mark was hungry so we went to get some food.

I felt anxious about a lot of things; was I doing the right thing by leaving Tom? Matt could look after himself and he loved Tom very much, so I began to relax. Ahead of me was London - would I find a job? That was frightening. Something else was worrying me. I would be staying with my friends, Carol and Khalid, at first, but after that, it wouldn't be easy to find a place in London. I could feel the tension build up again. I was miles away in thought, so I didn't say very much.

"Are you all right?" said Mark, cutting his egg, watching the yolk as it oozed and ran over the chips and beans, taking a quick glance at me now and again.

I stared at him, half-smiled and said, "Yes, I'm alright, just thinking about things." I couldn't confide in him, I didn't know him. I was going to have to sort it out myself, but I always did anyway.

"Yes, you'll be all right, there's lots of jobs, yes, you'll be alright," he said. I smiled again – he was a nice man in his abrupt way.

"Shall we go outside and get some fresh air?" Mark asked.

"Yes. Why not?"

In the far distance we could see Dover and the white cliffs. I didn't know whether I felt happy or apprehensive or both; I didn't know what the future held for me, my emotions were mixed.

We arrived at Dover, rolled off the ferry and the ramp leading down from the boat.

"I'm home." I half-grinned to myself, and mentally kissed the English ground.

Mark and I stopped at customs and were out before we knew it. It would take two hours at least to drive to London. When I got out of the car in Putney in London, I thanked Mark.

"Give me a ring sometime. We'll go to a pub or something."

"Will do, and thank you again."

I stood there for a minute. I looked up and there was a blackbird singing in a sycamore tree, welcoming me home.

Chapter 5:

London and All

I looked for a phone box and rang Carol. "Where are you?" she asked.

"Putney High Street."

"That's ten minutes away; I'll put the kettle on."

When Carol opened the door, hanging on to her bright red skirt was her little boy, two-year-old Saffron, a delightful chubby child with brown curly hair. Carol still looked about eighteen.

Down the dark hall came Khalid's voice. "You made it then, well done." He was a plump and indolent Egyptian, with a dark moustache, with brown eyes half shut and bare feet. He welcomed me with a sloppy kiss.

"You're in the small room," Carol said. "I painted it a few days ago, that's why the hyacinths are there, I don't think it makes any difference." She giggled.

"Very nice, I hope you didn't do it just for me."

"No, not really… let's go to the kitchen and then you can tell me your news."

***

I knew that Carol and Khalid's place was only a stopgap, and so I spent the next day looking for a job. I returned to my temporary home very tired. Nevertheless, I had a job as an agency computer operator; it was boring, but it would do for now.

That night I phoned my mother. "I'm back! How are you?"

"OK, apart from my arthritis."

She'd had arthritis for at least ten years, as did her mother.

"I've managed to find a job with an agency, in an office in Clapham," I told her. "It's nothing special, but it will do for now."

"I may have found you a flat as well," she said. "Give my friend Felicity Hambleton a ring, say who you are, she may have something; she can only say no, can't she?"

I thanked her very much, and though I was tired, I rang the number immediately and introduced myself. Miss Hambleton told me she did have a vacant flat, and so I made an appointment to see it the next day.

The flat was in Rosedale Road, West Dulwich, a leafy part of London. I rang the bell and two minutes later I heard footsteps and lots of dogs getting louder and louder.

"Yes?" said the woman who opened the door, a whippet under one arm and looking me up and down, observing me closely.

"I'm Emma Cook... Mrs West's daughter," I said, smiling and stretching out my hand. "I've come to see the flat." I withdrew my hand when the woman didn't respond.

The puzzled look on her face disappeared when it dawned on her who I was.

"I am so sorry! Of course, do come in." She smiled. Then she turned around and, looking down, flailed her arms in all directions and shouted, "Back! Back, all of you! Let her come in, for goodness sake." Five dogs had come to the door, wanting to know who was there.

Miss Hambleton put the whippet under her arm, and marched off upstairs, followed by the dogs, who were turning their heads to look at me. I followed her upstairs, as I smiled at the dogs; the flat was on the first floor.

In the small sitting room, the Ibizan hound immediately jumped onto the settee, bouncing up and down and looking at me as if to say, "Nice sofa, do you want to try it?"

"Down, Kasha," said his mistress, with authority, and the dog obeyed. I quickly stopped stroking the dog, and smiled at Miss Hambleton.

After viewing the small light green kitchen, tiny green bathroom with a shower and equally small green bedroom, we returned to the sitting room, where Miss Hambleton and I sat on the sofa, and the dogs sat on the floor. The Ibizan hound was close to Miss Hambleton, his adoring eyes watching her face; in return she was very gently stroking his head, whilst talking to me.

I said, "It's lovely, and I can pay you two weeks rent now if you like."

"Very well… when do you want to move in?"

"I would like this weekend, if that's possible," I replied. "A friend of mine was kind enough to put me up for a short while, but this is a find; thank you so much."

"You're welcome, I know what it's like in London," replied Miss Hambleton. "This weekend then… my first name is Felicity. Here are your keys."

"Thank you… I'm Emma, Felicity. See you on Saturday." I walked out into the low sunshine and turned around to say goodbye, but the door had already shut.

Chapter 6:

To and Fro

Matt was impressed when I phoned from my flat to say I had found somewhere to live and a job. "Wow, you have been busy then. You've got work and a flat in such a short time. Well done." It sounded almost patronizing, but I knew he meant it.

Why didn't he say something similar, when I was there?

I missed my son and I rang him twice a week or even more, imagining him in the sitting room with his blond hair, always wondering whether I was doing the right thing.

Tom told me enthusiastically, "We're having another football team. It'll be better than the last one, which was gruesome. The new one, I'm in it!"

I smiled to myself and told myself that he'd be all right.

I missed my dog Buddy, too, who had gone everywhere with me. Apparently now he ran up to every woman with blonde hair, thinking they were me. Knowing that really upset me. But what did I expect?

I managed to earn enough for my rent and going out occasionally, as well as paying for a fortnightly trip back to Holland with a bit left over to save. I would see Mark four or five times a month, to be sociable. I only knew Carol and Khalid, the couple downstairs and Felicity. London can be a lonely place.

∗∗∗

Mark was taking me back to Dordrecht, and out for meals or to pubs once a week. On one occasion we went to Eastbourne to see an old friend of Mark's, called Ginger, in a pub called 'The Fox'.

I liked him immediately. He was a kind, gentle giant, with ginger hair and a matching moustache. I wasn't a great drinker, and the men were talking about their times together, good and bad. The more they chatted the drunker they got.

"Do you remember when we turned up at your place at breakfast time?" said Mark. "I was the worse for wear, Pam and the children came into the kitchen just as I had buried my head in a bowl of cornflakes."

"That's why you're banned from our house." Ginger shook his head and grinned, before taking another gulp of beer.

Eventually, I drove back to London from Eastbourne, while Mark slept, but he woke up when the car stopped. "Are we there yet?" he asked, bemused, wiping his face with his hand.

"Goodnight, Mark," I said, getting out of the car.

Looking up at me, he said, apologetically, "Sorry, Ginger and I go way back and we always get drunk." He was slurring his words. He slowly drove off. Bump, bump, bump, twenty yards or so, he was off.

What an idiot! I thought. I hope the police don't catch him.

Chapter 7:

The Start of the Affair

Both Mark and I had commitments elsewhere, but nonetheless we began to get closer without either of us noticing, a touch on the arm here, a brush of the shoulders there. We met almost three times a week, and we were getting closer and closer. I found Mark was a tactile person and I gradually warmed to him, almost without realising, even if he was intoxicated fifty per cent of the time.

Ginger came up to London. Mark and I met him at Kings Cross, and he had three tickets to see *Phantom of the Opera*. I was delighted and Mark was obliged to go too.

After the show the men were dying for a drink, so we sat in the corner of the pub, with their pints of beer and a glass of wine for me.

"What did you think of the musical?" asked Ginger.

"Wasn't it lovely? It was very sad and lovely. Sarah Brightman has a beautiful voice. Thank you for taking me," I said and smiled at him.

"What about you, Mark?"

"It was all right I suppose," Mark said. "It's wasn't my thing, but as Emma said, she has a nice voice and she kept it going, didn't she?" He was embarrassed, I could see it by the colour of his cheeks! He had never seen a musical or anything like that, and he was staring straight ahead, not glancing at either Ginger or me.

"Your round, Emma, isn't it?"

"Oh yes, sorry! Same again, Ginger?" I hurriedly stood up to go to the bar, but as I did so, I tipped my bag upside down. I knelt on the floor to pick up the contents, and Mark bent to help me.

He found my lipstick between the legs of a chair, and held it out to me, nothing was said. I slowly took the lipstick from Mark, but I wasn't looking at lipstick, I was staring into his eyes, for a moment that seemed like forever. Then Mark helped me up by my arm and I banged my head on the table. I rubbed at the spot where I'd hit it – suddenly I felt as if I was suffocating.

"You alright, Emma?" asked Ginger.

"Yes, it's just been a long day, I suppose." Putting my hat on straight, I glanced at Mark. There was a strange feeling in the pit of my stomach like an ache, good and bad at the same time. But I smiled at Ginger.

Mark and Ginger decided we should all go back to Ginger's hotel for a nightcap; the hotel was two minutes from the pub apparently. In the lift, I could feel Mark close behind me, I could barely breathe, and I closed my eyes until we reached the third floor.

He leaned over, and whispered in my ear, "Wakey, wakey, we're here." I opened my eyes, and followed the men, until we reached Ginger's room.

I asked Ginger if I could lie down. I needed some sleep.

"Of course, help yourself." He waved at the bed.

I must have gone to sleep in an instant, and before I knew it, I was waking up to see the light of a new day coming through a chink in the red curtains. I could hear a blackbird singing above the noise of the slow-moving London traffic. There was only a light on, where the voices came from. I found my shoes and joined the men.

I went to the mini-bar, desperate for a cup of tea or coffee, but there were no teabags or coffee on top of the fridge. The four cans of lager were gone! No milk, and only a lonely bottle of wine in the fridge.

"I think I ought to go," I said.

"Not until you've had breakfast," Mark said, flustered. "I'm famished, don't know about you." He had a forlorn look on his face, as if he wanted to know what was going through my mind.

I felt awkward looking at him; I didn't know where to put my eyes. I said, not looking at him, "I suppose I am a bit peckish."

I put my coat on, and the three of us went out into the chilly morning air.

There was a delightful smell of fresh coffee coming from the first café we found. We went in. I ordered scrambled eggs on toast, and a cup of coffee to wake me up. Mark and Ginger had the full works: beans, sausage, bacon, eggs, mushrooms, fried bread and disgusting black pudding. A shiver went up my spine when I thought of it!

I sat opposite Mark, who, with a gentle grin on his face, was looking at me.

Ginger noticed it as well. "Silence is golden, but my eyes still see," he sang and he smiled. It brought a smile to my face, as I quickly glanced at him, and got on with my scrambled eggs.

When we'd finished eating, Ginger said, "I'm going to the hotel to collect my things, what about you two?" He looked at us both, putting his knife and fork side by side, before standing up.

"Yes! What are we doing, Emma?" asked Mark, also standing, pushing the chair underneath the table, and resting his hands on the back of the chair, waiting for me to reply.

"Home I suppose," I said, and smiled. "Lovely seeing you, Ginger, it was a really nice night, thank you." I kissed his cheek and put my arm around him affectionately. "See you soon, I hope?"

"Yes, nice to see you Ginger," said Mark. "Give me a ring when you're coming to London next and we'll get together again, but not a musical, if you don't mind!" We laughed.

We went on the underground as far as Brixton, and then caught a bus back to my flat. Our conversation was minimal and consisted of 'yes' or 'no' responses. We reached his car which he had left outside my flat. Separating without saying anything, he drove off down the hill.

When I arrived at the front door, I met Felicity, who was taking the dogs out for a walk.

"Hello," I said, smiling at her and the dogs. They recognised me, and they were wagging their tails, and I responded by patting them.

"Where's he going?" asked Felicity, peering in the distance over the top of me.

"I don't know, back to his flat, I suppose," I replied, turning around to see the car in the distance.

When I got inside in my flat, I reached for the telephone, and quickly phoned Holland. But there was nobody in. I desperately needed to talk to Matt and to hear his voice. We were getting farther and farther away from each other, and I was aching for Mark.

***

I went to bed and drifted off to sleep again. When I awoke it was twelve o'clock. I had a shower, and made myself a cup of tea. I rang Holland again; no joy there.

Eventually, I got the bike out; maybe a bike ride would do me good. I rode down the hill to Dulwich Park; the birds were singing, it was a beautiful day. I breathed in, and smelt the freshly mown grass; perhaps it had been mown that morning!

A blackbird was looking for worms on the grass, when I drew close to him. He flattened his wings when I almost touched him, and quickly he flew to the nearest branch. The blackbird looked at me and screeched, and I giggled inside.

I saw two people talking on the bench, and the girl was tittering too. There was something in the air; a child screamed with delight, as an older child chased her. There were dogs chasing one another. I could hear the echo of horses trotting on the other side of the park. It was a lovely spring day and my senses were alive!

Mark's car was hidden by the trees. I didn't know it was there until I was almost on top of it. The thumping music came out of nowhere and I didn't know whether to go forwards or backwards. I was standing in the middle of the road, the people in the car were now impatient and tooted loudly, followed by another toot, and another toot, until I made up my mind which way to go.

I chose to go forwards. Mark saw me and our eyes met for a long moment; I was fixed there for a moment.

Nervously, I waved and at the same time I made my mind up. I got off my bike, shaking as I did, lying it on the grass, and in eight steps I was in the car.

"I wondered how long you'd take to find me," said Mark with a grin, his left arm almost touching me on the shoulder; that touch went all over me. We looked at each other for a moment or two, then I closed my eyes and we shared a long and very hungry kiss.

"I think we ought to find some place quieter than here, don't you?" he said when we surfaced.

I nodded and grinned, my eyes flashed; I knew what I wanted, even though it was stupid and foolish.

Mark got out of his car, picked up my bike and put it in the boot, and we drove out of the park, only we were heading south west, over the Chelsea Bridge and the Thames. Five minutes later we were at his flat.

***

That evening, we had a long meal in a curry house in Herne Hill. We found a window seat, and held hands over the table like adolescents. It seemed like we were the only people around, even though the restaurant was full, but it didn't matter at that time, I was eclectic, and elevated; I'd never felt like that. We gazed at each other, and laughed quietly and smiled over the menu.

Later Mark drove to the corner near my flat, took my bike out of the boot and handed it to me; we shared a long kiss goodnight. I was in a haze, but the ache had finally left me.

Chapter 8:

The Partings

Matt and Tom came over from Holland to England. The day after we went for a picnic; there was silence as we sat on the green, with the hot sun in the sky. Once thirteen-year-old Tom was out of earshot, I had to tell Matt I was having an affair.

It was a shock; all that Matt could say was, "I see." He stared at me with a vacant look, but he didn't question me, he knew I meant it.

Tom came back from feeding the birds, and realised something was wrong with his parents; he didn't know what it was, but something told him that things were not right. His mum and his dad seemed too wrapped up in their own worlds to think about him. So, it was a sad and awful time for everybody, particularly Tom.

Two days later, it was very awkward, when Matt told Tom that he and I were parting. I would be staying where I was and Matt and Tom would be moving to Brighton. Tom would go to college eventually in Brighton.

After four and half years in Dordrecht, Tom liked it there in Holland. I felt very remorseful, but it was too late to do anything about it, they were here now. The Holland adventure was at an end.

***

Mark had split from his second wife Maggie and he needed to earn more money, so he went to Saudi Arabia. The money was great, twenty thousand a year, which was quite a lot in the 1980s, but it meant that I was on my own most of the time.

I had a German friend who knew both Matt and Mark. She thought I should live on my own for a little bit! Lotte had met plenty of people like Mark and she told me to stay well clear.

"He was a drunk to start with and he's leaving the second wife, apparently, that tells you something, surely?"

She began to speak more gently. "Please listen." I turned around, leant back on the work surface and folded my arms, gazing at the floor. I knew she was right.

"If I were you, if you want to split from Matt, obviously it's up to you, but I would live on my own for a couple of years; you haven't ever been really alone have you?" she said, staring at me. "Now is the time to do it, live a little, have your son staying with you, you can do anything. I mean it; think about what I've said." It was sensible, but it went over my head, because I was in love.

Lotte looked into my eyes, shook her head, and said, "You didn't hear a word. I must say, for a thirty-seven-year-old, you are really rather foolish and immature."

***

Every week Mark and I wrote to each other, forgetting Lotte's advice to me. I really liked getting mail from him. Foolish as it was, I felt I was really in love; I knew it was love, or maybe lust, or both? I didn't know the difference. I was still very naive.

Every four months Mark came home for fourteen days, and I took time off from work; it was wonderful to have him home. I even picked him up at Heathrow by taxi at five in the morning, not wanting to miss a second. I was besotted, love-struck and obsessed; nothing else mattered!

We borrowed a campervan to go to Littlehampton, and we chased each other on West beach to Clymping. Sunday evening there was a thunderstorm at sea. We watched from the car. It was thrilling and exhilarating.

Another time we were near Guildford in the Chantries, where we had a take-away. We made a fire, talked about the meaning of life in all its forms, sitting near the fire; he opened his arms invitingly with a blanket. Then, we didn't talk, we had done our talking, we just stared at the fire.

In the morning, we walked up the beautiful Chantries and after having some breakfast, we went down and round to the tip of the North Downs.

***

Monday came, my mind was filled with emotions and feelings. I watched him, and thought, 'He's going back in three days' time.' I had in my mind how many days there were, until there was one day left. Then he was gone.

In the beginning, I didn't question my relationship, all I knew was I loved him, that was it. He was a drunk, however, a good drunk, there was nothing bad about him, not really. I know he really wound up people sometimes, but that was all.

Later, he liked teasing me and was mischievous at times. He enjoyed looking at other girls, naturally, and to make me jealous I suppose; it worked well. I still didn't know myself at all. But I did love him; whenever he would walk into a room, I'd get foolish, but in the end, it was futile!

***

One week after Mark went back, I had a persistent headache. It went on and on, so I went to the doctor. He looked at my throat and eyes and said, "Right! I want you to relax for two weeks."

I said immediately, "I have a job, I can't…"

"I'll give you a note. You must rest." He still wasn't saying why, but he was insistent.

I did that for seven days, then I got bored and my headache had gone, so I went on the bike again to Putney and to Carol's home. It wasn't as far as I thought, and it was a nice day, the close of summer and autumn not far away. The leaves were green with touches of brown, orange and yellow around the outside.

Carol was out, so I trundled back, past Wandsworth, Clapham, Brixton and finally West Dulwich, where I fell into bed. I could feel my headache only slightly. I should have listened to my body, but I didn't!

Chapter 9:

Crystal Palace Lane

The one thing I was thinking about a lot was buying a house, where Mark and I could live. I wrote to him suggesting that if we bought a house with enough space, we could rent out a room or two, but we would only have to find the deposit.

Mark wrote back and said he would think about it, then, five days later a cheque came in the post for six thousand pounds. His only stipulation was that the house must be near the South Circular.

I was thrilled. After work I scoured the estate agents' windows, I pored over the homes for sale in the local paper and on Saturdays and Sundays I went to look at them.

One Saturday I found exactly the right house in Crystal Palace Lane, not far from the South Circular. It needed a lot of redecorating, but it was cheap. It was an old Victorian house, with a musty smell because it hadn't been occupied for a year.

This is it! I thought, standing in the dining room, seeing the paper peeling off the wall practically in front of me. I was standing on a brown and yellow carpet, which led to the stairs, and the same colours and pattern went on and up the stairs.

"How much is it?" I asked the estate agent, Brian, as we were walking to the kitchen.

Brian looked flustered as he was looking down and peering at the folder with him. "Oh! Err… forty-five thousand pounds." He raised his head and smiled at me. He was young and inexperienced; this was the second house he'd shown people round. This was my first house, and I was excited!

"I see," I said. I still felt thrilled at the thought this could be the one.

We went upstairs to the three and a half bedrooms. The first bedroom near the stairs was dark because the light in the room was the right side of the house. The bedroom had blue flowers on the wallpaper, bare boards and there was not a stick of furniture in the room, only heavy curtains. I walked to the window and looked down to see the wild garden, and beyond there was a steel fence, past which was the railway line.

We went back out to a hall that was dim even with a light on. There was a second bedroom also on the left hand side, smaller; this was dingy with bare boards again, and it had a wardrobe in the corner with one door shut and one door open.

The bathroom was even bleaker; the taps were dripping into the bath and it was rusty where the water touched, although the tiles around the tub and the sink were very white. The curtains were grey and had holes where the moths had been. The old wallpaper had been white, but was now turning grey and brown. Next to the bathroom, there was a green and white papered wall and a toilet.

We came out again to the dim passage, turned right, back tracking. Brian opened the door to the third bedroom. Immediately, there was sun shining through the hall and the large room, over the roofs of the houses. The sun also picked up the yellow strips of wallpaper, and the heavy curtains which didn't match. Pink and green tiles stood out against the black surroundings of the Victorian fireplace. Through the window there was a view of the small garden and the road, where cars were parked.

Finally, after a quick look at the smallest bedroom, I said, "It looks like a cupboard." I stared at Brian. But I still found myself enthusiastic and excited again.

Brian nodded and smiled.

I grinned and said, "Please, I'd like to see the outside and the garden."

"Of course, please, come with me."

At the end of the kitchen there were three steps down; on the right there was another toilet and beyond that was a small room, a work place maybe? On the left hand side, there was a green door leading out to the garden. Brian released two bolts and turned the door handle. He opened the door and we went out into the fresh air, releasing us from the slightly musty smell of the house.

I walked to the back of the garden, looking at bluebells, daffodils and crocuses; they were just emerging. There was an old apple tree that shaded a quarter of the garden, and had tiny apples on it. Somebody had been looking after the garden. It was enchanting!

Then I clapped my hands with exhilaration when a train went by, very fast. "Oh!" I said, the sound almost knocking me back; I burst out laughing. I knew I wanted this house.

I could see rusty gardening equipment through the greenhouse glass. I tried to open it, but the door was stuck. Brian came to help me but I said, "Okay, another time perhaps."

Two minutes later I was standing in the kitchen. I said, "It's a lovely house, but it needs a lot doing to it. I will need to think about it and I'll talk to my partner."

"Okay, Mrs Cook," said Brian, giving me his card. "I'll wait for your call."

I phoned Mark to tell him about the house. "If it's the one you want, go for it," was his response.

That afternoon I rang the estate agency and made an offer for forty thousand pounds. Brian rang back and said, "The seller won't accept that offer, but he will go to forty-three thousand."

"Done," I said, and I patted myself mentally on the back.

I found a solicitor, Ms. Christine Baker, who said it would be advisable to have two names on the deeds.

I went along with her guidance.

Eight weeks later, I packed my few belongings in my grandmother's large trunk and two or three pieces of furniture from the flat in West Dulwich, and unpacked them in Crystal Palace Lane, a quarter of a mile away.

I had two or three work colleagues over, with my friend Carol and the neighbours around to welcome me to my new house, then things carried on as normal, and I started to decorate.

I didn't make friends easily and I felt quite lonely, although I did have lots of friends outside of London, particularly in Brighton and Guildford, and I had work colleagues. I had only two friends in London and an acquaintance of Carol's called Jenny. We had met at Carol's house one evening and we met a week later in Putney for coffee and went around some charity shops.

***

Mark was coming home for good, and a month later, we went on holiday with two of his friends, Gerhard and his wife Edith and their two children. Gerhard was a grey-haired Dutchman with glasses and a potbelly, because he drank too much, but he spoke six languages. Edith was much younger than him. She came from South Africa, where they met.

We followed Gerhard and his family to the South of France, were we pitched our small tent on a camping site by a river in the Dordogne.

The next day it was hot. I lay on the grass in the sun and went to sleep, until I was woken by Mark. "You can't sleep now, we're going to look around. There are some lovely villages and great vineyards here! Come on."

The four of us and the children hurried through the beautiful villages, then slowed down and stopped in the vineyards.

The only people who had a great time were Mark and Gerhard, who had had seven days of heaven, drinking wine and going to the grape growers. Gerhard spoke most of the time because he knew a little French, though Mark didn't, so he just nodded when he thought it was appropriate.

I was relieved when after a week Mark and I returned home.

Chapter 10:

Waking Up

I am awake now. I can hear a blackbird singing from a long way off, mixed up with the usual hospital noises. Some people are snoring and nurses are talking quietly in the low light down the ward. It is dawn.

How did I get here? I can't remember, my mind is in a haze; gazing around me left and right, the light is low.

All of a sudden, I feel thirsty. I can see the bell on my right-hand side, although I discover that I can't lift my right arm, let alone press anything. However, it doesn't register, and it doesn't occur to me that there is anything wrong with my arm. Anyhow, lifting my left hand over my body, I manage to press the button.

A minute later, I can hear feet coming towards me, and a nurse appears.

"You're awake, are you?" I suppose is it the Irish lilt in her voice, but I find her reassuring. I need a drink.

The nurse reads my mind. "I bet you want a drink?" She smiles and I manage a weak nod and a half smile back. I do want to talk, but I don't know how to.

The nurse pulls the bedrail down; she is talking and taking a cup of water from the bedside cabinet and holding my head. I drink it all. I try to say thank you, though I still can't speak. However, I don't think about it much; I am desperately tired even though I have been a sleep for how long? I have no idea, although, it doesn't matter anyway. I close my eyes.

"Don't worry, just go back to sleep," says the nurse, and she walks softly away from the bed.

***

Later, the clattering and banging on the ward wake me once more; I try to sit up, but it is no use. I press the bell with my left hand, knowing that my right hand is useless.

"Do you want to sit up?" asks another nurse who has just appeared and is standing by my bed, fiddling with the sheets.

I nod.

The nurse pulls me up, and she puts a pillow behind me, then tidies the bed again.

"Do you want any breakfast?"

I nod, feeling like a child.

Five minutes later, she comes back with soggy cereal and one slice of white toast with butter and marmalade. "Cereal first!"

I smile, looking at the cereal and the white toast, and, suddenly, I'm feeling really hungry.

The nurse lifts a spoonful of cereal towards my mouth. I have difficulty opening my mouth, because the right side of my face is numb. I feel the right side of my face with my left hand, gazing at the nurse, and raise my left eyebrow in a question.

"You've had quite a shock; I'll let the doctors tell you, meanwhile, we need to get some food inside you, if you can?" She's smiling.

I frown at the nurse; what she is telling me? I don't understand.

But I pick up the spoon in my left hand and lift the cereal to my mouth. Half the food goes into my mouth, the rest dribbles down my chin.

The nurse says, "Ah! You're left handed - that's helpful. I'll come back in ten minutes to see how you're doing."

What does she mean?

***

Mark has been in the shadows for a while, he tells me, watching the nurse. I can see that he has tears in his eyes.

In fact, he still can't believe it, and he is numb and shaking, and he's looking at me. Do I look odd? Apparently there is a droop on the right-hand side of my face. But he pulls up a chair and awkwardly sits down, taking my left hand in his.

I try to speak, and it comes out as gobbledegook and babble, however, I am still smiling, with not a clue what has really happened to me.

Mark is listening to my voice, and he goes white, and slowly half withdraws his hand; seemingly, it is more than dreadful, and horrifying to hear me, and he turns away for a moment. I can see the tears again are pricking his eyes, but I still don't know why.

***

"The stroke will get better, however, how long, I cannot say, it's up to her."

The doctor is studying me, smiling at me. I am half-smiling back as he continues. "It will be a long time, maybe five years, probably more, the rest of her life perhaps, we don't know, who knows? She is young, that is the good part of it."

I really don't understand, and I look at Mark for any answers, although it is too much for Mark to take it in, as well as for me to comprehend. It is the worst, worst situation he has ever been in, he can't believe it, he is almost paralysed, as I am paralysed, paralysed with my speech, and the right side of my body, paralysed.

Another older doctor arrives, and shakes hands with Mark. He is sitting on the other side of the bed, his left arm crossing my legs. I am half smiling at him as if he is coming to talk about the weather, however, there is indeed a storm brewing - he is the bringer of bad news.

"Mrs Cook, have you heard of a stroke?"

He waits for me to answer. I'm confused - that's the second time I've heard the word stroke used. I know old people have strokes. I can't work it out, how can it happen to me? I wrinkle my forehead, staring hard at Mark, who is ashen and grim-

37

faced. I turn back to the doctor and the smile is vanishing from my face, and I realise that he isn't joking. Who would joke about that kind of thing anyway?

The first of many tears fall onto the sheets; five days ago I had been a whole person, with everything to live for. Now, I am incapacitated and disabled on one side, with a lop-sided mouth and an arm that is turning inwards and is hanging against my chest. Fortunately, I don't yet realise how bad my situation really is.

Chapter 11:

Little by Little

Five days later, I am tucked away in the corner of the ward, listening to Chris Rea's 'Driving Home for Christmas', but it's really hot outside, the beginning of June.

It seems I haven't got a care in the world, as I am even dancing in the bed, until Mark turns up. He always looks shocked when he stares at me, even if I am beaming and smiling at him. Maybe that's making it worse?

A while later the nurse brings me my dinner, and puts a fork in front of me. I'm ravenous.

Halfway through the meal, a friend of mine, Joanna, arrives. Somebody had told her that I had had a stroke, but she hadn't really thought about it, or what it meant, until now.

I smile at her, and half my dinner falls out of my lop-sided mouth.

Mark is sitting on the other side of me, not wanting to say anything. He is embarrassed about the way I look.

He says a few words to Joanna, as she sits down, squirming as she watches me intently, and her eyes never leave my face. She can't believe it and she doesn't know what to say to Mark. So, there are stilted sentences from her and him, and gobbledy-gook from me, and after half an hour she leaves. I don't see her for several months.

***

At last, my mother comes to see me. I have been in hospital for what seems like ages, but I suppose she is here now.

While she is shocked about the stroke, she hides it very well. My mother is made of sterner stuff, apparently nothing fazes her. I try to give her a half-smile, and try to say, "I will beat this in six months." But I don't know what I'm saying, and I don't yet know how serious things are.

The nurse comes over to tell me I have a dentist's appointment at two that afternoon. She turns to my mother, smiling.

"You can go too, I'm sure you want to."

"Of course."

But when the nurse leaves, she whispers, "I can't be away for long, Fay is on holiday so I'm looking after the dogs."

My mother feels guilty, I'm sure, though there is no need. Later, she leaves me at the dentist, uttering her goodbyes and hurrying away.

***

Mark comes every evening after work at six o'clock on the dot. He is lonely and he is still shocked and dismayed every time he sees me. He must be wondering what has happened, how I am now almost a shell.

Just ten days ago, the day before the stroke, we were in a pub across from Herne Hill station. She was alright, wasn't she? he must be thinking.

I am unconscious as to the thoughts and feelings of others, because I just can't deal with another person's angst. I have my own problems to think about in my unclear and vague brain.

***

The doctor comes around about ten o'clock. Apparently, they have decided to do an M.R.I scan, and he sits on the bed, putting his arm across my legs again.

He is talking loudly. "You are going downstairs and you are having an M.R.I, some time today, okay?"

I smile and nod. "Okay." I am not deaf, and I still have a sense of humour and I half-smile at him.

I am laughing and crying, laughing and crying a lot. I don't know why.

At two o'clock a nurse arrives and she takes me down to have the M.R.I.

The technician tells me not to move when I am placed in a tiny vault, a strange noise all around my head, and a minuscule shake.

Thank goodness I am not claustrophobic, and after ten minutes it is finished, and I am back on my ward.

The next day, several doctors come around, at ten o'clock on the dot. The same doctor tells me, again in that loud voice, that they can't find any reason for my stroke. "I hope we'll get to the bottom of it," he says, but they never do!

He smiles, and moves on to the next bed.

***

I have had what is called an infarct or infarction stroke, an ischaemic stroke, there are many types of stroke, mainly caused by a blockage in a blood vessel in the brain. Some people call it a brain attack.

***

Every evening Mark and I go to the pub and we go out for a meal once or twice a week. Mark has found a good Indian restaurant near the hospital, where the waiters quickly push the chairs out of the way - they put me and my wheelchair instead at centre stage.

The other diners stare at me when I'm eating my food as it dribbles down my chin, especially when I'm trying to smile at them; somehow it makes things worse.

Mark leans forward, looking right and left. I am still chewing like baby, and Mark says, very gently, "Wipe your mouth and chin."

I look around, smiling, and almost all the people, when I glance at them, turn around and get on with their curries, and talk too noisily to their fellow diners.

***

Right from the beginning, I have to do exercises in the afternoons. At first, I wasn't concerned, even though I couldn't walk for about six weeks.

However, I talk to the almoner, and she says, "You must try to get up, to walk, because, only you, only you, have the determination to get yourself right, even if you succeed seventy, eighty or even ninety per cent. Do you understand me?" She is staring into my eyes.

I understand what she is telling me, and my willingness to get better overrides everything else, even though, at the time, the significance and importance aren't that clear to me.

I go down to the exercise room, clinging to the physiotherapist, Sylvia, who is slim and blonde-haired, who tells me, piercingly, "Do what your left is doing and carry that to your right."

Sylvia demonstrates what I'm supposed to do. So, we go up and down stairs until I get it right, holding on to the banisters with my left hand, so I do not fall – all with a lot of help from Sylvia.

She must be strong, I think.

"And one, and…where is the right leg….thank you."

Almost singing: "And one and…. where is the right leg… right leg… That's the right?"

Again and again, and again, so on until we reach the top. "And one and … two… one and … two, well done." Down again to the bottom of the makeshift stairs.

The thing is, I won't remember tomorrow the sequence of today.

"Now rest." And she is smiling. "Good."

I am able to get out of my wheelchair in about six weeks, though I still have a long, long way to go. I cannot speak, only gabbling; although I know what I want to say, I always get it completely wrong.

***

One day I have to phone Mark because I want him to bring in another set of nightclothes. "Ell, arrk, I... arrk, I... aa. Ell, arrk, I, I... Ssh-i-t!" I put the phone down hard, tears running down my face, and I keep hitting the phone box with the phone, in utter, utter exasperation.

I turn in my wheelchair and ride down the hall all the way to my ward, sobbing and punching the wheel with my left hand, veering all over the place.

"Wh...y me, wh...y me, wh...y, wh...y?" I am trying to say, but my speech is so strange, when people hear me, they turn around and watch me pass by with open mouths.

***

It is late at night and the lights are low, I want a pen and paper to write something down. However, I cannot get the male nurse to understand what I'm saying, about a piece of paper and a pen. Eventually I give up trying, and I turn my back to the wall, with tears and frustration in my eyes, and finally go to sleep.

***

Social Services would like to see Mark and me, and we are to go into the little green room with them.

Miss Goodchild, tall, erect and with glasses, is there, and her assistant Susan, dark-haired, short and young, the nurse, Amy from U.C.H, Mark and me.

Miss Goodchild, smiling, asks Mark several questions about our home.

I can see this is difficult for Mark; for one thing, he doesn't want to be here, all these questions, questions and more questions.

I am an onlooker, and participator as well, because it is all about me, though it is over my head, some of it anyway. I am sitting here meekly, nobody asking me about my concerns at all, thank goodness. I guess they know I can't talk, still I smile now and again, and that is enough.

Susan asks, "Is it possible to get the shower downstairs for Emma in the bedroom? Do you think it's big enough?"

I gaze at Mark, nodding and smiling; he doesn't see me however, he is thinking it through, looking at the floor.

Then he looks up, and he is uncomfortable; he clears his throat and he raises his voice. "Yes, it's big enough to put a shower in there. No problem." He smiles quickly at Susan.

Miss Goodchild asks, "Where is the toilet, is that on the ground floor?" She is looking at him sideways, as if she has an opinion about him.

"Yes, next to the kitchen, you go down to the toilet which is on the right-hand side. Then, the back door is on the left where you can go out to the garden."

"So, the kitchen, that's on the ground floor?"

"Yes."

"Mm…Well! That's it for the moment," Miss Goodchild says. Her complexion is deepest pink, and, looking at her watch, she asks, "Any questions you want to ask me, Mr. Hurst?"

Mark smiles at Miss Goodchild.

I can tell he doesn't like her one little bit. She's in that category, very direct, and she doesn't like him either, and she is only doing her job, that's all. So, I am uncomfortable for her and him; all this is because of me.

"Well, here's my card if you need some support or anything, Mr. Hurst."

I look at her and smile. She doesn't notice me at all. I wonder what she's thinking about the both of us.

Without regarding her, Mark takes the card and says nothing, just gives her a nod.

Miss Goodchild smiles at everyone as she stands up, and Susan and the nurse follow her out of the little green room.

Outside, Mark relaxes. "Ah! I think it's time for a beer."

***

One Saturday in June, Mark drives me home for the afternoon. The weather is dull and grey with frequent downpours, and my tears, like the rain, pour down my cheeks.

But I am thrilled to see the sights of London again. There are lots of people in cafés, looking in shop windows and going to the cinema or the theatre.

When we get to the house, the curtains are closed, so it is dark inside. I manage to ask Mark to take me out into the garden, where I start to cry again.

I'll never dig the garden now.

I look at Mark through the window; he can see me weeping. He can't bear my crying any longer, so he backs away from the window, and finally takes me back to the safety of the ward.

On the way back I stare at the crowds of people, but this time the excitement is gone. I am just thinking, "I used to be like them, but I'm different now, so different."

Chapter 12:

The Guinea Pig

One Monday afternoon, two students doctors come to see me. I am sitting in my wheelchair, and one of the students bends down to me, smiling. "Can we use you as a sort of guinea pig this afternoon, on the stage in the auditorium?"

I nod and smile at the two of them, not really hearing the words 'guinea pig' but, wanting to oblige anyway. All the world is a stage.

One of them grabs the handle of my wheelchair and we go along the corridor, turning left into the lift to go down to the ground floor and outside.

This is exciting, I tell myself, and I feel a smile coming over my face, as I close my eyes for a minute. There is a slight breeze and I can hear the trees shimmer. I open my eyes, putting my left hand up to shield myself from the very hot sun. We move quickly through another building, through the corridors, until we reach our destination.

There is an audience of students at the front of the stage. I hear them laughing and talking, with doctors on the platform, waiting for a body, a young female body who has had a stroke.

I hesitate and I shy away with my face, turning to the left, because the student is wheeling me on to the stage anyway. I can't do anything about it, so I just go with it, but I don't like it at all.

I catch the eyes of one student in the front row. She gives me a half-smile as she sits down. What is she thinking about me? And I smile back.

The rest of the students around her are quietly laughing and talking in the front row, as she sits there waiting with a serious face. Suddenly though, she is laughing, her neighbour evidently saying something funny.

The lights dim overhead and all the students sit down and are hushed, and the stage lights are on me. I can only see the front row of the audience, the girl stops laughing, I can see in even the dim light, she has a serious face now, not like ten seconds ago. I feel awkward and I'm frowning - my smile is gone as well. This isn't how I was imagining it.

The students who brought me are behind the chair, and another older doctor is smiling at me and patting my hand. I look up at him with my half-crooked smile.

Then I turn to the consultant, who is talking about me as if I am an object, and a number.

"Look at her mouth, it's turning down." He is holding a ruler against my face whilst he is talking. I flinch away from the ruler as I stare up at him, with his thin lips and light blue eyes.

I feel the tears coming, and I wipe them quickly with my left hand before they fall. But he does not notice me at all. I am just a woman who has had a stroke, that's all.

"The arm," he picks up my right arm and drops it. "You can see she has had a stroke." I might as well be a piece of meat, that he is showing the students, and the girl.

I am trying to smile at the students, to convey to them that I am still a human being like anybody else, but inside I am weeping; I feel wretched. I don't want to see the audience like this, so, I try to cover my body like a cocoon with my dressing gown as much as possible with my left hand. I look down, staring left and right. Oh! The shame of it!

After ten minutes, the doctors have finished with me, and the student is pushing me back, without saying anything, through the corridor, out into the fresh air, though I don't notice anything, it's a blur.

A blackbird is skimming across me now along with his alarm call, although I cannot see him, because my eyes are full of tears. All I see is a black thing flapping his wings; I know his cry and I want to cry as well.

Bloody doctors!

47

I am back again in the ward, still reeling with contempt and disgust at the two students. I am hurt and silently raving mad, and it is abuse now. However, in those days it was acceptable.

One of the students bends down. "Thank you, for helping us enormously." One look at my face tells him I'm not amused.

The student gets up quickly; he is painfully uncomfortable, with bright red cheeks, and he hurries away to joining his colleague. It is not his job to placate me.

Two minutes later the young nurse comes by. "There you are. I thought you'd escaped." She is almost laughing. But noticing my faraway look, and my tears, she lowers her voice, and on her knees and looking up at me, gently smiling, she asks, "Are you okay? Do you want a cup of tea?"

I look down, not answering her, still with my eyes filling with water. The nurse brings me a cup of tea anyway, and she rests her hands on my shoulder for a moment. "Dinner won't be long and your man shouldn't be long either." She looks at her watch and the door, and I'm still crying.

Chapter 13:

Tom

It is a lovely afternoon in late June, five weeks after my stroke. A young man is walking down the ward. Tom, my son, who is sixteen years old, and he is nervous about seeing his mother. He knows I have had a stroke, but that doesn't mean anything to him necessarily. He thinks only old people have strokes, 'So it can't be that,' he is telling himself. However, he doesn't know what to expect.

I am dreading his arrival too; I am more than a little bit nervous. 'Surely he knows, but he's never seen me frightful before, certainly nothing like this. Somebody must have told him the bad news.'

There is Tom, holding a bunch of flowers. I shakily smile at him and I wave feebly.

"Hello, Mum, how are you?" He bends down and kisses me, as he gives me the bunch of flowers. I take them shakily, and give him another quick smile, putting them on the bedside table.

I thank him with a smile, no talking necessary.

But tears well up and I search for some tissues.

"How are you?" He is almost shaking and I can tell he wants me to look at him and speak normally, naturally.

I pluck up the courage. "Yo-u… alo-ne, din't… Dad br- you?"

"Pardon?" He grows pale.

I am sure Tom wants to run away; this is awful for the both of us. He sits down in the chair next to the bed.

Shaking his head, not looking at the pattern on the floor, he says, "No, no… Dad's working."

He can't believe the gabble I'm talking; it's still ringing in his ears and he lifts his head, and is gazing at me in shock, that he hides with a wonky grin.

He clears his throat and starts again. "Dad has known for a fortnight, though he's only told me in the last two days, because I said I was going to see you, obviously, then, he told me that you were in hospital."

On the opposite side of the ward a white-haired old lady is snoring; she is covered in white sheets and a blanket, and with the merging of her white hair and the white sheets we can only just see her.

Another lady in her sixties is next to me; she is a chatterbox, though she is quite adorable. Her name is Anne. She doesn't seem to care when I talk gobbledy-gook, and get things wrong – she treats me the same way she treats everybody else. She doesn't know it, but she's a confidence builder.

"This is your son?" asks Anne in her East End accent. "Nice! He's the spitting image of you."

A quick smile, and I nod; nevertheless, I'm watching Tom, as he gazes round the ward. Dreadful, poor boy, he is almost a man, yet only sixteen. Anne carries on talking though, beaming at Tom and saying, "Your father comes every evening."

She means well, I smile, I can't find the words to explain to her. What does it matter anyway? I think.

Tom and I half grin at each other, and I glance towards the door; there is no question Tom is staying here, I know that, so my eyes are showing him the way out and to the garden.

"I…am go…ing out, see y… l…a…ter, we a…re go…ing to the gar…den," I whisper to Anne.

Anne is smiling, and she is almost waving in front of my face. "Right!"

"Right," says Tom, unlocking the wheelchair forcefully, and wheeling me out of the ward.

Tom hasn't got used to me talking gibberish either! Will that ever change? I ask myself.

It has been raining, but now the sun is coming out. I take deep breaths, smelling the fresh air outside. We find a place among the flowers and some trees. There are roses and perinea, and the big flowers are having difficulty lifting their petals up, and the leaves are dripping after the storm. There is no sign of the blackbird and the traffic seems far away.

I watch Tom's face and reach for his hand. "So-r-ry."

Tom smiles, but he doesn't look at me.

"How long are you staying in this place then?"

He looks terrible.

"I don't know."

There is silence.

"How's Mark?" asks Tom, after a while. "Dad told me, and I suppose Mark told him."

He doesn't really like Mark; he doesn't understand why his mother has got tied to a drunk.

I brighten up at the mentioning of Mark's name, sitting up and smiling, until I realise that I am talking to my son. I wither in my chair, physically and mentally.

"Okay."

Nothing more is said, and I smile at him self-consciously.

Tom smiles back, however, I can tell that, inside, he is deeply hurt. He is very angry, and I know he thinks that Mark is to blame.

"Has Grandma been to see you, or anybody else?"

"Yes. But, she has to go ba-ck fe-ed the dogs!"

I start to giggle, which is infectious and makes Tom relax a bit. Although, it's not really funny.

"I-t lov… se-ein-g y-ou!" I put my left hand on his arm. "O-ur fa-mi-ly, ho-n-stl-y! Yo-ur gran-d-fa-ther, I am ha-v' nt nt see ing im." I shake my head and giggle again.

After a while, Tom looks serious. "I suppose we'd better go in now; I must get back to Brighton, but at least I don't have to feed any dogs."

Tom and I nearly burst out laughing, knowing there will be tears before long. I want him to go but I want him to stay.

We go through the gardens and return to the ward. Tom kisses me on the cheek and my hand reaches up to his face, as if I want to hold the kiss there for a moment or two. I am crying inside, though not outside, I am forcing myself to smile. I go with him to the lift. He is turning and waving, and I am silently saying, "Goodbye." The lift door slowly shuts and he is gone.

I come back into the ward, and I look around my bed. Somebody has put the flowers in a vase, they are sitting next to my bed. I am smiling and crying all at once.

***

The first horrendous meeting with his mother. I imagine him carrying his anger with him on the train. The shadow of the woman who used to be his mother, the impact is horrifying and he must have been shocked to see me like that. He didn't know then it was going to be a lifetime getting used to this other woman. I sit there for an age; maybe he will come back, but I know he won't.

Chapter 14:

Standing and Walking

I am still doing exercises every day, and my face has gone back to almost normal, although my leg is still weak and my right hand is very poor. However, I am using the bath myself instead of needing a hoist and two nurses to lift me. I walk to the shop close by in the hospital to get a paper.

Very gradually I am able to take more and more steps – ten yards, twenty yards and then fifty yards. However, it is always with a bad limp, my gait awkward and veering to the left. I am frustrated because I know that I could be doing more, to make me whole again.

I can walk ten yards, and I can see the lift coming up from the ground floor at six o'clock and I hope it is Mark. So, I stand opposite the lift, and coming out of the lift is Mark. Mark doesn't recognise me, because I am standing up straight, so he just walks by, looking as if he has the world on his shoulders.

"Hel-lo Ma-rk." I am behind him, and have a grin on my face.

Mark turns around, surprised! "Oh! Well done." He's surprised, and he grabs my hand and kisses me on the cheek, without smiling.

"Go-od, I wan-na si-t dow-n." I drag him up the ward until I reach my wheelchair. I sit down, closing my eyes and letting out a sigh of relief, rubbing my weak leg.

"Are you alright?" Mark asks.

I nod. "Y-es, y-es, I- am o-k."

"Oh well! We should celebrate you walking."

Anything to have a pint, I think. "Wh…y no…t?"

Mark pushes me hurriedly into the lift and out into the fresh air, and round the corner, there is a pub!

He buys a pint for himself and a half pint for me.

"Cheers, well done," he says, and we clink our glasses together.

At times like this, when the sun is dropping in the sky, I feel close to Mark. The end of June is a lovely time of year, but suddenly, my tears begin to fall, again. Mark gets his handkerchief out, and hands it to me, but he's not looking directly at me - he's glancing down to his watch.

I have finished crying, and Mark is staring at me, gently shaking his head. "What on earth are you crying for? Look, you're walking, that's a start."

I can't do anything more than nod, and blow my nose and wipe my eyes; I know he's right. I'm facing a long process and the very thought of it makes me miserable. We sit in silence for a while, gazing into space.

He's looking at his watch again.

"Go-in-g so-me-wh-er-e?"

"No, no, just a pint with the boys in Clapham."

I struggle to nod and smile, the tears trickling down my cheeks. Mark pushes me back to the ward, with the usual peck on the cheek. "See you tomorrow," he says but he is barely looking at me.

It is almost dark now and the nurses are busy with the pill round.

Chapter 15:

Lemon Meringue Pie

Ann Potter, one of the social services team, wants to know whether I can cook for myself.

"What would you like to make?"

I grin. I'm thinking, Cook by name, but I can't find the words to end the sentence.

"Lem-on mer-in-g p-ie, my s-on likes that."

Miss Potter giving me a sideways glance.

"Okay! What ingredients do you need then?" asks the social worker, with her patronising smile.

I glance at Miss Potter and then gaze at the ceiling, listing the ingredients from memory, as the social worker writes them down.

"Is this right?" Miss Potter asks me; she doesn't trust me completely.

I glance at the list. "Yes, th-at rig-ht."

"Right, twenty minutes."

When she returns, I take the plastic bag from her and get to work in the ward kitchen. I roll out the pastry, with one and a half hands, my hand veering to my left with the pastry. I cook the pastry for twenty minutes or so; I found rice and grease-proof paper in the cupboard, to hold the base down.

Then I fill it with a mixture of lemon juice, and lemon peel, egg yolks, sugar, cornflour and water. Finally, I pile on the meringue with the whites of the eggs, and a sprinkling of salt, with about four ounces of sugar.

I never weigh anything, neither did my mother.

I put it back in the oven to cook on a medium heat, for twenty to thirty minutes.

When it's ready, I proudly put it on the table. The social workers, including Miss Potter, nurses and doctors alike, all follow their noses, to see what I have achieved.

It's gone in a flash and they all declare, "That was delicious, well done."

"I'm sure you could get a job here in the kitchen," says one of the doctors, smiling.

I feel uplifted. "Tha-nk y-ou," I say, even though they are a little bit condescending; they mean well. I know it is a good lemon meringue pie.

***

The next day the almoner invites me into her office.

"There's another hospital that has a dedicated stroke unit - Charing Cross Hospital. You may have heard of it?"

"N..o."

"I think it will do you better than here. So, I have made arrangements for you to move early next week. We've done all we can, and the other hospital has everything you need to make yourself better."

I am delighted and can't wait for the following week.

Chapter 16:

Charing Cross Hospital

The day I'm due to move, I wake up with a feeling of optimism. I shower and clean my teeth. Then, I begin packing my belongings, even the cards I have been sent, and I look at them again. I'm smiling, though it's only six in the morning!

Mrs MacDonald comes around at seven with the last breakfast; she gives me the usual, cereal, two pieces of white toast, a hard-boiled egg and marmalade.

"I hear you're going to Charing Cross Hospital; is that right?"

"I am!" I'm smiling. "Yes, I am lo-ok-ing fo-rd it, I ca-nt wa-it."

"Oh! I will miss you, well, good luck anyway."

"Go-odby-e Mrs Mm-acDonald. Tha—nks!"

***

The porter who is picking me up is supposed to be here at ten o'clock, but he is late, it's a quarter to eleven. But finally he arrives, complaining about an accident on the way, so he is cross! Not at me, but at the hold-up.

"Are you ready? I'm running late, obviously this accident has put me back." He can see I'm ready, and he looks around the ward. "Anybody else?"

"Yes," says Mrs Kinkaid, in her soft southern Irish accent.

Apparently, she had her stroke on the bus going home to her husband. I imagine it was as much a shock for him as it was for Mark.

I nip back to Anne, and give her a hug. She is smiling, and her eyes are filled with tears, but her strong hands are on my arms.

"Get well," she says gently, looking into my eyes. "Get well, now go on."

"Tha-nk-yo-u. Yo-u to-o!" I am kissing her, and I know I won't see Anne again, and my eyes are full of tears again.

However, there are tears of joy as well, as I walk towards the porter, who will take me to the next phase in making me well again. I look around the ward. The nurses and sister are busy with patients; they already said their goodbyes half an hour ago, which were short but warm.

I lift my left arm up high and wave and smile at Anne for the last time, mouthing, 'Goodbye.'

In the van, I look at Mrs Kinkaid. "It's ex..cit..ing, is..n't it?"

Mrs Kinkaid pats my hand, but then turns her head, gazing out of the window. She doesn't want to talk.

It takes about half an hour to drive to Charring Cross hospital in the London traffic. London is magnificent - I find it exhilarating with the hubbub and the noise! I desperately want to be part of it again. Again, there are tears of frustration.

The stroke unit is set away from the hospital itself. I can't wait, and I limp to the lift which takes us up to the first floor.

Up and away. I am grinning to myself, but, as the lift door opens I stare with disbelief at the scene before me, my mouth dropping open, as I cower at the back of the lift.

There must be a mistake. All the patients eating their lunch are old; but what did I expect?

"Come on, dear, you're here," says the driver.

Mrs Kinkaid is waving at me and beckons me. "Come on, love, it will be alright."

At that moment a starchy nurse comes to rescue me. She speaks to me gently, but forcefully. "You must be Mrs Cook."

She comes over to the lift, and says, forcefully but gently at the same time, "Come with me, it will be alright." She puts her arms around my shoulders firmly, and looking into my eyes, she says again, smiling, "It will be okay."

I feel my fingers releasing my hand from the bar, and we go out of the lift. I am so nervous and shaking, my leg is limping dreadfully, and I am gaping at the old people; they don't notice me. Some have food falling down the outside of their mouths and chins; they don't feel it, as I don't feel it. Visibly, they have had a stroke as well. Oh! It is a nightmare because I am awake!

"Here we are," the nurse is announcing, in a very matter of fact kind of a way and she opens the door.

"I thought you would be better in your own room. Have you had lunch yet?"

I shake my head.

"Do you want anything to eat, sandwiches or something?" asks the nurse, watching me more closely.

Again, I shake my head forcibly. "N-o." I'm remembering the old people I passed a minute ago.

"Right. I'll tell them you're here."

I tentatively unpack, and again, tears spring to my eyes and run down my face.

Ten minutes later there is a knock at the door. "Hello."

I turn around, wiping the tears with my hand. He has a white tunic, and he is stepping gingerly further into the room. He looks concerned.

I'm sitting down on the bed, with the suitcase behind me, bits and pieces everywhere, watching him.

He is half way into the room, "Are you alright?" he asks, although he can see that I'm not. He takes a handkerchief from his top pocket and, as he is giving it to me, asks me, "Do you want to take a walk in the grounds? There's a space where we can talk."

I stare at him! He has a sympathetic air, maybe I can listen to him? But, no way, I can't live here. I will give a Mark a ring, he can fetch me, but he won't do that, will he?

At present, I am feeling angry, even hostile. However, I nod.

"Shall.. we ..go ..then?"

"I forgot to say, my name is Roger Wells. I'm your physiotherapist, and you are Emma Cook?"

"Th--at's ri-ght."

"We'll go out to the grounds, they're very lovely this time of year."

I follow him, walking as fast as possible with my wonky gait, still knowing I will have to come back.

Out in the garden, Roger guides me to a seat beneath a yew tree. I look down and I see a blackbird digging for some worms. I stare blankly at the bird, and I think, 'He can fly away, I can't.' Clearly, I am feeling very sorry for myself.

The bird seems to read my thoughts, and, once he has had his fill, he is flying away until I can't see him anymore, disappearing behind the trees. I feel very sad, and low; the tears flow down my cheeks again.

I keep hold of Roger's handkerchief; it's almost comforting.

"You're not used to yourself yet; I've seen this often. However, you are very young, and you will fight, honestly."

I stop weeping, and dry my eyes and look at him, trying to listen to what he is saying to me.

"Why... happn me, wh... me?"

"It could happen to anybody, even a baby. You were very unlucky. There is nothing on your scan to indicate the reason for your stroke. But gradually you will feel better; it is up to you, you do know that, don't you?"

I nod.

"What I mean is, you have two choices, you can sit here, do absolutely nothing, and in ten years you will still be sitting here, exactly as you are now, or you can fight it with a good brain. I imagine it is a good brain, and I bet you like a challenge too, don't you?"

I raise my eyebrow, indicating that he is being condescending.

Roger clears his throat.

"Ten years from now you can pat yourself on the back and say, 'I did it.' I imagine you have a lack of self-worth at the moment, though that will change, believe me."

I acknowledge his words, and turn my head away to think.

"Te...n ye...ars is a lo...ng ti...me. I sa.id to m...y mo...ther, chuckling, I wi...ll be ou...t of he...re in si...x mo...nths."

"You're grieving, and you will continue to grieve for a while, six months or even a year. It's like... you've lost someone, do you know what I mean?"

I nod. "I sup...po...se I d...o. " I can talk to him. "Fort...unat...ely I li...ke chal...len...ges."

I stare at him and smile.

"That's it really, it's up to you! I can see an active girl who is damaged with a stroke. Only your will will get you back, Emma, only you."

He pauses, then continues gently. "You will never reach a hundred per cent, maybe eighty-five per cent, but who knows, nobody knows, it's up to you."

I give him his handkerchief back in exchange for his profound words. I will never forget what he has said.

"Tha...nk yo..u."

We walk back through the garden. I'm exhausted and go to bed.

Lying there on the bed, I think about Roger's words. "It's up to you."

✳✳✳

Mark comes to visit me, every day as usual, dead on six o'clock. He can see immediately that I am not happy.

"You don't like it here do you?"

I shake my head forcefully! "No, go-od me, but old people and I..." I burst into tears and try to finish. "Ther not-hing wro...n ol peo-le, but I am no-t ...ol-d."

Clearly, I'm already forgetting what Roger had said to me.

Mark stares at the floor until my tears cease; he is not finding this easy at all.

"Come on, don't get on your high horse. I think there's a pub round the corner, we can talk about it there."

In the pub, he tells me that he's created a shower downstairs in the house on Crystal Palace Lane, which Social Services asked us to do. Also, he's added a short banister by the two steps down to the back door and the toilet.

"Somebody from Social Services came to inspect it, and it's okay apparently. Anyway, she was quite satisfied."

I am impressed. "Ni...ce... you, tha...n yo...u."

I rest my hand on his arm, but he takes it away immediately. Something tells me I shouldn't do that. Why?

Then there's a silence and then I blurt out loudly, with no hesitation, "I wa...nt to go ho...me."

I glance at Mark's face and I'm not sure whether he's pleased or not; all he can say is, "I see."

He looks slightly worried. Well! He has fitted the shower for me, he told me, a minute ago, although I am afraid of his answer and afraid of his response.

However, there is none; he silently wheels me back to my room, without talking at all. The silence it's awful, and he gives me a cold kiss as he saunters away without turning round.

"Se-e you to-morrow, Ma...rk?"

"Yep." He waves carelessly, not looking around, the lift door opens and closes with him behind it.

I have terrible feeling in the pit of my stomach.

***

At nine o'clock every day, I am supposed to go downstairs and mix with the other patients for some gentle exercises.

They are damaged like me, either mentally or physically, or both. While we are all in it together, I can't cope with them for too long.

I am surprised I don't see Roger in any of these sessions, after all, he is supposed to be my physiotherapist. So, I go outside after about twenty minutes, and I sit beneath the yew tree and weep.

Every day I cry my eyes out, until the smell of food and the pangs of hunger take me back indoors.

I have been in this hospital for four weeks now, and Mark is doing nothing to get me out of here. I suppose he is scared.

***

One day after lunch, I'm looking out of the window when I notice someone standing next to me.

"Hel-lo," I say, smiling.

"Hi," replies the woman; she's about fifty, and she stubs her cigarette out in the ashtray. She begins to talk to me, but not to me; she is gazing out of the window, and I'm looking at her, and listening to what she is saying.

"There's nothing to do here, absolutely nothing. I've been here for a whole year. I was told all sorts of things, you wouldn't believe it, but they don't do anything."

"Wh...y... don... go ho-m?"

The woman stares at me. "I ask myself the same question every day."

She walks away after that short conversation, and, as I'm grasping what she has told me, she goes out of the swing doors, and disappears.

***

That evening Mark and I go to the pub as usual, and he starts the cold conversation with one word, "So."

I draw my breath in. "I to-ld y-ou, we-eks ag-o, w-a-n-t go ho-me!"

I am holding my breath again. "Th-ey ar do-in-g no-th-in-g. I wa-nt to go h-me. I wa...s tal..king to awo...ma, sh...e sai...d exa...ctly th...at. Do noth...ing. I...am twid....dlin my thu....mbs in he...re fo...r not...hing."

Instead of crying, I am angry, but I am really scared of what Mark is going to say.

"I was waiting for that," Mark says, not looking at me. "When?"

"N-ow! I hav-e se-en Ro-ger, w-ho su-pp-ose be m-y ph-ysio, s-aw me wh-en I'v-e co-me in, and a fe-w fn-e wo-rds, and on-ce or tw-ice, bu-t th-at it.

"Wa-nt … go ho-me …now. Wh-at use st-aying? I have… be…en .here… fo…ur we-eks…f..or … no-thing?"

Mark has never seen me so very incensed and irritated. I am shocked at myself as well; until now I always worried about what Mark would say.

However, he puts his hand on my shoulder and says, "Shh, don't worry, I'll arrange it."

However, I suspect the moment he has secretly been dreading is here.

Chapter 17:

Home

On the day I'm supposed to go home, I'm excited and nervous at the same time.

Mark has said he will arrive about six o'clock to pick me up, and he is usually on time, though seven comes and goes and he is nowhere to be seen, nor does he turn up at half past seven, eight o'clock or nine.

I am beside myself and the sister has to give me a pill to calm me down, and knock me out as well. The nurse has seen it all before, and the pill works wonders, and I sleep all night.

It appears that Mark calls later that night to speaks to the nurse, inebriated, saying that he will be there in the morning.

She tells me this as she gives me my cup of tea in the morning.

"Mr. Hurst will be over shortly; I would drink this and get dressed, if I were you."

So, I wash, and hurriedly dress, feeling a little bit apprehensive, and as I am coming out of the bathroom, I see Mark sitting on the bed.

"Hello. Got your things packed, I see." He doesn't look up and he doesn't apologize for not appearing the night before either!

He is shaking, because, I imagine, he had lots of whisky chasers the previous night.

"Y-es…rea-dy ta g-o," I say anxiously, with a half-smile.

Abruptly, Mark picks up my suitcase and walks toward the lift. It seems he doesn't care whether I accompany him or not, but he is waiting for me by the lift all the same.

I quickly shake hands with the sister and the other nurses.

"Thank you for all you have done."

I hurry after him, as he stands watching me by the lift. I am self-conscious, not knowing what he is thinking, making me limp more than ever.

But, there is a surprise downstairs; there are some of the physiotherapists including Roger, who are waiting to say goodbye to me, though they really haven't done enough for me, particularly Roger.

"Don't forget your exercises," Roger says, trying to smooth the situation, almost seeming like a friend.

I scrutinise Roger's face, as if I'm saying, "Which are?"

Roger is taken aback with my brusque answer; his cheeks are red and he pauses. "Well! Think of polishing a table and stretching and walking about with a heavy bag."

I am sniggering inside, and slowly walking to the door, as Roger calls out, "Please get in touch with us if there are any problems."

When Roger and I went to the garden when I first got here, Roger gave me some extremely first class words, which will stay with me for a long time, and I am thankful to him for that. However, I look at him and the physiotherapists, and imagine they are feeling very, very guilty. They have not spent time with me, not a jot, and I am very disappointed; I thought physiotherapists would do so much for me. I am the youngest one here, I need the exercises to get me going; that is why I am here!

Roger has apologies written all over his face, as I turn and go through the door, and I am on the way home.

***

I am so excited to get home that when we draw up at the house, I throw the car door open, and wait for Mark to help me onto my feet. He hastily does that and then he walks up the path, unlocks the front door and steps into the hallway, waiting impatiently for me to catch up.

Mark can't look at me, he is looking over my head, as I carefully tread over the threshold, then, turning right, follow him into our bedroom.

"Here's your shower," he says brusquely, showing me the changes he's made, which are remarkable.

"It… lo-ve-ly, tha-you, Mark," I say. I want to kiss him, but he is flinching, and pushing away and quickly walking through the hall and kitchen. I follow him as quickly as I can.

Mark points to the three stairs at the end of the kitchen. "You know there are steps, and some banisters so you don't fall, going up or down. Anyway, I'm going to work now."

Mark squeezes past me and I get the smell of him, the faint odour of drink on his breath. He can't wait to get out of here, and he turns quickly, not looking in my direction, and says, "I'll see you when I see you."

Alarmed, I look down at the ground. "I tho…ught y…ou wou…ld be in a…ll d…" My speech is carried away to the ground, and bounces up again, so, no sound to speak of. I can feel the tears in my eyes.

Picking up his crash helmet, ignoring me, he rushes out of the front door. I am sensing that Mark is feeling awful, that he can't deal with me. I'm beginning to think that he wants to completely dispense with me, but he can't throw me out.

Thank goodness for the solicitor, Christine Baker.

That's why he is so hostile towards me, because he loved the old me, not this new and damaged one. He can't talk about it either, there is nothing to talk about, and he is wallowing in drink, and with the rest of his thoughts, which never get near the surface.

He revs up his motorbike and he is off without another glance in the rear-view mirror. I close the green door in a haze, then I start to sob against the corner of the wall behind the door.

I'm shocked at how cold he has been towards me, and I feel numb. What do I expect, Mark is young, thirty-seven, but I am young as well, I am only eighteen months older than him, it's nothing, though I am damaged and dented like an old car!

I cannot move and I feel frozen around my body; my left hand is wiping my tears, and slowly, slowly I walk back to the bedroom.

The house is really quiet, though I can hear people and cars going by outside my window. I unpack my bag and put my things away in the wardrobe. I look at the clothes already hanging there, and flick through them, remembering what I had been doing last time I'd worn them. Again, tears are falling gently off my face, and are falling on to the floor; I half-smile, staring at the dresses.

Half-an-hour later, I go to the kitchen and peek into the cupboards. There is tea, coffee and cocoa in one and various tins in the other.

I make tea, realising that this the first time I have made tea for a long time. I gape out of the window to the garden which I long to be standing in, so I finish my tea in two gulps.

I look around in the garden. The grass has grown a lot and the rusty tools are still in the greenhouse, just as I left them. I walk to the back of the garden, and glimpse up and see the apples on the apple tree.

There will be a bumper crop of cooking apples, when they are fully grown. Staring across, between the railings, there are lots of green and black blackberries as well, apple and blackberry pie! I realise how hungry I am; I haven't eaten anything all day.

Turning back to the house, I wonder whether anyone is watching me from the nearby properties; most likely they're not at home, they're at work earning money paying their mortgages. House prices have already risen quite a bit since we bought ours.

I make another cup of tea in the kitchen, and gazing in the fridge, see it is well stocked with eggs, bacon, mince and lots of salad and bread. 'I won't starve at least, thank you, Mark.'

I make myself a sandwich and am sitting down to eat it when I hear the door open.

I hope it is Mark, but in the pit of my stomach, I know it isn't; it's probably Jack, our tenant. I walk shakily to the hallway.

He is half way upstairs. "Hel…lo, Jack," I say, and he turns around.

He doesn't know I have just come out from hospital, because Mark has forgotten to tell him, and for a moment he doesn't recognise my voice or where it is coming from.

"My goodness." He comes quickly back down the stairs.

"How are you?" He is thrilled to see me, I can see that.

I am smiling as he is grabbing hold of my hands, and kissing me on the cheek.

"I… am ok…ay. I… b..ck ear…ly… the hos…it…l u…less, so I ca…m th…s mo…ning."

There is silence for a few seconds. Jack obviously wasn't aware how much the stroke has affected my speech. I can see that he is dismayed, but he doesn't let it show too much. Instead, he smiles and asks, "Where's Mark? Isn't he with you?"

He can see I've been crying, but I don't answer.

"Oh dear." He doesn't know what to do. "Is there anything I can do?" He takes off his coat and puts it over the end of the banisters.

"We can go for a walk some time. What do you think about that?"

My face completely lights up; I am smiling through my tears. "Y… y…es wy n…o..t. Wh…at abo – ut tomorrow?"

"Do you think you can make it to Brockwell Park?"

I am feeling better now; I take a deep breath in. "Is… n… ce be… home. Do yo…u w…nt te..a?"

"Hmm …why not," says Jack, raising his eyebrows, and following me into the kitchen. I know he is staring down and seeing how weak my right leg is, and how fragile I am.

I turn around when we are reach the kitchen. Jack quickly looks up, as if he has a guilty secret; he sympathises very much with me, I am sure.

I make tea for Jack and me in silence. Jack is watching me with affection. He breaks the silence and says, genuinely, "As I said, anything you want, just ask, won't you? Don't hesitate!"

***

Mark doesn't get back until one o'clock in the morning, by which time I am in bed and sleeping, until he comes in, then, I am awake. I don't ask where he's been, anyway, I can see he is drunk and so I let him think I am asleep. He tries to get into bed without disturbing me, but an elephant would have done a better job! Within five minutes he is snoring, and I am awake, weeping silently.

Mark wakes at six forty-five and he is gone.

Chapter 18:

Look at Myself

Stephen Hawkins says: Don't be disabled in spirit as well as physically.

***

I am slowly getting up. I am seeing people going past my window, and cars and buses too as I peek through the blinds.

The dressing gown is on the bed, and I reach for it, and put it on. Then I walk to the kitchen because I want a cup of tea. Jack is upstairs, I can hear him, apart from him there is no one else, and down here, I am here alone.

I put the kettle on and make tea and carry it through to my bedroom. I sit down on my bed, and switch on the T.V. and watch the news, but it's not particularly interesting, so I switch off.

I shower and go back to the bedroom. And I start to cry again. 'What are you crying about now?' I ask myself. 'Everything and nothing. Bloody everything!' I smile.

Now I look into the mirror for the first time and for a long time, and I see a kind face, my face.

The droop is gone, thank goodness, and I drop the towel. I am naked. My stroke has not damaged me or deformed me when I am standing still. Though, when I walk, I limp and I'm humiliated by that, because I'm not used to it.

I think there is a distinction between damaged and deformed; it's almost the same in the dictionary. I call it the two 'Ds'. It doesn't matter really, I am alive, I suppose?

I am alive! I can speak, and I hope that in the days and months to come , though it will be stilted and stiff, it will improve.

It is called dysphasia, I have read; a lack of coordination in speech, owing to brain damage. It's hard to express.

I am remembering the first memory of my stroke, I could not say anything that made any sense. It's still a bit gobbledygook, however, my speech is getting better, slowly.

I know I will have to have speech lessons as soon as possible back at the hospital, probably King's College Hospital, that being the nearest one to me.

I look at my right hand, and my right hand is not as good as my left. It's shorter than the left, because it's tighter in the elbow. Thank goodness I am left handed so that doesn't matter so much, but it would be lovely to be able to hold a knife and fork, instead of only a fork.

I get frustrated tying my shoe laces up and doing buttons up on my blouse or coat, for instance. I curse and swear, blaspheming to God. There is no dysphasia when I do that, I notice!

I have not worked out whether or not I am a 'cripple,' or worse, 'handicapped'. I don't like that appalling word. Thinking about it, I realise nobody else can use it, only me and maybe those closest to me, but I don't like the two words anyway.

Another shudder goes down my body and again my eyes fill with tears. Maybe, 'disabled', I can eventually handle that, I think, as I examine myself before the mirror.

However, there is still something in me, beyond my stroke, my desire and lust for life that was given to me when I was born. I stand, facing the mirror for another minute, then I smile, and turn, and I put my clothes on.

Chapter 19:

A Good Friend and Family

It seems that friends go away like leaves in autumn falling from a tree.

***

At one o'clock in the afternoon, Jack appears in the kitchen.
"Are you ready?"

We go out of the front door; it is lovely, another beautiful day. I pause on the pathway, and take a deep, deep breath outside of London's air, closing my eyes and smiling, enjoying the sunshine.

Then we turn right out of the front garden, and go towards the park, very slowly. Jack is much older than me, so he is not so fast in any case, thank goodness.

I recall the last time I had been out, with Mark, while I was still in hospital. Mark had pushed me in my wheelchair to a pub; it felt different then.

I am still very anxious when I am passing people; I feel they are looking at me, with one leg normal on one side and the other leg limping, going all over the place. Thinking about it now, I realise people are just getting on with their own lives, and I don't think they notice me at all. However, though, still it doesn't stop me nervously watching them.

I can see Brockwell Park, Herne Hill, fifteen minutes later, and the park looks inviting, with people walking and talking. There are screaming children and barking dogs, although I don't feel ready for the park, I feel it in my bones, and I am standing there staring.

I turn to Jack. "Cou-ld w-g–home?" I am almost crying but still holding it in, and I turn round and walk as fast as I can go, with my wonky leg, until I reach home.

I get my breath back, holding on to the front door. I close my eyes again. I let go of the door, my mouth agape but soundless. I feel crushed.

Jack comes in to the garden, saying nothing, just opening the door. Once inside I quickly open the bedroom door, swiftly close it, and fling myself down on the bed, sobbing!

***

Over the next few months Jack becomes like a father to me, and he never asks about Mark because he knows anyway.

Jack keeps taking me to cafés and restaurants, introducing me to other people, like Ella, who doesn't let my stroke bother her too much, and we become firm friends. Jack is trying to boost my confidence more and more each day.

He is in his eighties and smokes like a trooper, forty cigarettes a day at least. He drinks about four pints of beer each time he goes out to the pub, either in Herne Hill or Crystal Palace about three or four times a week. I go with him sometimes, particularly the pub at Herne Hill. He becomes a true friend.

Obviously, Jack is retired; he had a career as a sports correspondent at the Daily Telegraph. He knows Tony Hancock, the lovely funny magician Tommy Cooper and other people like that around Fleet Street. There's 'The Coach and Horses,' 'The Old Bell', and 'The Punch Tavern', and many more, I am sure.

But he has a sad side. I know he got divorced and after that he came to live in my house for one reason or another, one of them being that he disliked being alone.

He passed away about ten years later whilst out crossing a road near us. He was visiting a friend in Croxted Road; he was crossing the road, when he has a massive heart attack and died shortly after. It was a shock for me and everybody who knew him.

***

It is taking a long time to get on my feet again; I feel scared of anything and everything. It's about five years before I feel I can relax a bit, preferring to be alone unless I'm with friends. Although in my experience the majority of my friends visit only once and they don't come again. Except Jenny, who is very dependable and true.

Mark is rarely here; he leaves the house at seven and returns about midnight. However, his attitude softens when he realises I am not going to be too much of a burden. Evidently he thinks it is better not to protect me too much, so he carries on doing whatever he wants.

I may have had a stroke, but that does not mean that my intelligence and awareness are impaired. I am trying not to think about Mark, but, if he comes in to the room, and I haven't seen him for a while, I get jittery and nervous like a juvenile, still, fatuous and foolish.

***

My mother comes and visits me. At the front door, she gives me a quick kiss, no hugs, even though it's a long time since we've seen each other.

We stand there, awkwardly, and I stare at her. I notice I have a mouth like hers, but I have my father's eyes.

Mother starts off by saying, "How are you?"

"OK… Sha…ll w go in t…o th…e kit…ch…n?" I lead the way, because this is the first time she has ever visited Crystal Palace Lane.

"I can't be away for too long, obviously, because…" she says, sitting down at the table.

"Of th-e… do-gs, tha…nk y…ou for com…ing." I breathe out.

"Anyway, d…o…ou lik…e a cake or a sa…ndiche?" I am smiling at her, a wide smile because I am feeling guilty.

She sees the Battenberg cake. I know it's one of her favourites.

"Battenberg cake, thank you." She gives that half smile, not looking at my face, the smile is for me nevertheless. My mother is so shy, it is painful sometimes.

Inherently, I know I am a little bit like her, in many ways. I like her sense of humour, and her stubbornness. I am wilful as well, which is good, because I have a stroke to contend with. Maybe, vetzyme will do the trick as well; it was a 'B' vitamin for the dogs. I used to love them too, when I was a child, as well as the dogs. Good for their health, and their coats, and me, with shiny short hair, because, I think my mother wanted me to be a boy, as well as my father.

Then, something extraordinary is happening, for my mother says, "If there is no one to care for you, I will come up and care for you myself. What do you think?"

I can't believe it. Slowly and unwittingly, I smile and say, "Oh... Tha...nk you... bt the...re no nee...d reall...y, no ne...ed. Tha...nky...ou ve...y mu...ch any...way.

I am surprised, and speechless at what she has said, but I clear my throat. "Sha...ll we g...o out...side, I think the su...n is com...ing o.ut, muc...h wa...rme...r than he...re."

However, I am hot and humbled by what she is saying. I cannot remember her doing anything like this before, and I am very touched and rather embarrassed. She is putting me above her dogs. Astonishing!

We sit in the garden around the fish pond and stare at the fish. I realise they want feeding as well. They are swimming around and around, particularly the big grey and red one. So, I get the fish food from the greenhouse, and sprinkle the food on to the water. My mother and I watch the fish gobbling the food.

"Ho...w are th...e do...gs? An...y pupp...ies?"

"Jazzy's bursting, any moment now, I suspect it will be two days maximum, I imagine five or six pups, I have to see." Mum is smiling and laughing for a second.

After half an hour, we go inside. Mum is off to see her dogs, all seven of them, and maybe pups as well? I kiss her, and she screws up her face and kisses very quickly.

"Goodbye, you're doing well. I will come again, I don't know when, but I will though."

"Se...e yo Mu...m, lvely to see y...ou, goo...d...bye." I touch her arm.

The next time I see her in the house is years later, with Tom; in the meantime I go frequently to Cranbrook where she lives.

***

I want to see my father, and Mark is taking me, although he doesn't want me to go.

"He didn't come to see you in hospital, or even send a card. Why are you going to see him? You're too soft, that's your problem."

I know he is right, though I still want to see my father all the same, even though my choice may still have been inadvisable, and the visit is not a good one either. My father is shocked at how much his daughter has changed because of the stroke; he doesn't know what to do, and he feels bad about not coming to see me in hospital.

Mark is making him feel even guiltier.

Six months later, my father is rushed into hospital with a heart attack. Three times I go to see him, because when all is said and done I still love him. However, I don't think he is grateful for my visiting him.

***

He was one of those brave, brave men in the war, a rear gunner on a Lancaster bomber. The plane was blown up and he was the only one not to be killed.

Sometimes he would wish he'd died with them! His parachute was on fire and he tumbled down 300 feet.

He said, "God make it quick." Then he passed out.

My father landed in a field in France. His fall was broken by either wires or trees, and he woke up, confused, and thought he was in heaven. He was taken in by the French resistance very badly wounded, with a broken leg and shrapnel in his shoulder.

Mesure, Noel and the other resistance men felt very sorry for him, because, clearly, he could not run at all, and that meant they couldn't get him back on the plane and home.

So, the French resistance put him back in the woods, and the Nazis found him and transported him to Paris. They never knew where the French resistance kept their hideaway.

In Paris, they mended his leg and after moved him to a prisoner of war camp in Poland, via Auschwitz (he knew what happened there at that time), for a year, and he was twenty when the war finished.

Back at home, just before he returned to civvy street, the R.A.F doctor asked him, "Do you wet the bed?"

My father replied, apparently with contempt and disdain, "No."

The doctor smiled and said, "You can go," and ushered him out through the door. That is the only counselling he got; my father never got over his survivor's guilt.

He did however have a wonderful singing voice, and matinee idol looks. He worked for his father, my grandfather, for twenty years, in a coal delivery business.

Chapter 20:

King's College

I have to see a consultant, Mr Grieves, at King's College Hospital, at the end of September of 1986. Mark takes me there, and we wait for over an hour. Just as Mark is about to reach breaking point, a nurse calls my name.

The consultant looks at us, and I feel he is immediately summing us up. I can imagine him thinking, 'Lovely as she is, the stroke has knocked the stuffing out of her. He's doing his duty and nothing else, but at least he's still here. I wonder if the father or mother is around?' But he doesn't ask.

"Well," he says, looking at the report he has received about me from the previous hospital. "How did this happen? You're very young to have had this kind of stroke."

Which doesn't help, because I don't really understand. I give him a blank look.

I glance at Mark, who is also expressionless, and then I turn back to the consultant.

"Str-ess." Though it's not easy, it comes out in my voice.

"I see," says the consultant; he, like most doctors at the time, does not believe that a stroke can be caused by stress alone and some don't believe it at all.

Changing the subject, Mr Grieves half-smiles and says, "You're left handed I notice! That is fortunate for you for many reasons, isn't it?" But he doesn't tell me why.

Luckily, I know why, because the right hand is never going to work properly.

"Y-es," I reply, looking at and considering my left hand and the right hand.

"Now," Mr Grieves is speaking in a direct manner to me, and glancing to Mark and the papers again. "I've booked you in for physiotherapy twice a week for two hours, and half an hour's speech therapy starting next week, and a psychiatrist in a fortnight's time, okay?"

He is looking up to me with a big, big smile, because he knows that half-an-hour won't be good enough for me or anyone. But I just smile through clenched teeth.

The consultant is clearing his throat; maybe he knows what I'm thinking. He turns to Mark for any questions he might want to ask. Mark is shaking his head, but he tells me later that what the hospital is offering is a disgrace.

"Well, that's all for now, I'll see you in a month's time. Good luck." And he stands up, shakes hands with both of us, and he shows us out of the door.

***

When the time comes, I am allotted to a physiotherapist whose name is Anna. Anna is watching me, walking up and down several times, and then she pushes and pulls my leg and arm until she is satisfied what exercises I can do, both at the hospital and at home.

"What about we go swimming, what do you think?"

I nod and smile. I like Anna and I feel safe in her company. In my broken speech, I tell her Brixton pool is near to me.

"Okay, next week we will have a swim."

"Y-es, tha f-fine," I reply and I grin.

***

We have a swim on a Wednesday morning. There are children splashing about and piercing laughter, until the teacher stops them with a whistle.

It is warm in the swimming pool and I swim around in circles, until I get the hang of it; at least I am swimming even though it is round in circles. Then, I go backwards and forwards, across the swimming pool with Anna, who is excited and says, "Very good," and asks, "You are alright, you're not tired, are you?"

I shake my head. There is a bar around the swimming pool, which I can hold on to, and, splashing with my legs, I have a lovely feeling of abandonment. I cross the pool once, then, suddenly I am very tired.

I have enough sense to say, "I've had enough."

I take the bus home. I am immensely afraid, but proud of my achievement.

Though, sometimes I feel so wretched that I don't think I can't go on, and I tell Anna in tears that I would shoot myself if I has the mind to do it.

Anna is mortified and she asks a colleague of hers called Mrs Swan to quieten me down. Anna can't cope with me at the moment; one of her relatives has died and it shocks her as well.

Mrs Swan works as a receptionist, dinner lady, and a shoulder to cry on if needs be. She is very patient and she sits with me, until I have almost got the smile back on my face.

Mrs Swan lives around the corner from me and two or three times a week, I call in to see her. She keeps me sane and we develop a real friendship; she is like a mother to me, one of the best people I know, and her humour keeps me laughing all the way home.

***

Apart from Anna and Mrs Swan, I feel I am getting nowhere with the hospital. What is the point of having a speech therapist for half an hour? I need a whole day of speech therapy. It really frustrates me.

The first time Mark comes with me to the appointment. For half of it I'm in floods of tears, because the therapist asks so many mundane questions.

But eventually I am able to concentrate on the job in hand, however, there are only a few minutes left. In front of me are cards printed with words or pictures and I have to say what goes with what: pen and paper, needle and cotton.

"Where does the penguin live?" The speech therapist is smiling.

I feel like a little child, and I'm very angry. I shout, "Ant-ar-tic!"

The therapist jumps. "Goodness me! Well done, Emma," she says, her face red. She looks at her watch, then she stares at me, condescendingly, and with a wide smile says, "That's it, I'm afraid,"

***

I see the psychiatrist only once; she cannot make out what I'm saying to her. "What the hell am I doing here anyway?" I think, and do not make any more appointments.

Chapter 21:

Farringdon College

I have been told about therapy sessions at Farringdon College.

It is February 1987, nearly a year since I had my stroke. The sessions take place twice a week, for a whole day for young stroke survivors, Tuesday and Thursday, ten a.m. until four p.m.

"Wonderful," I think. "Something I can get my teeth into." My speech is better than it was, but the words don't roll off my tongue exactly. So, some more 'how now brown cow'. That's what I need, desperately.

***

Eight-thirty and it's rush hour, and I'm terrified. I get the number three bus to Brixton, then the overground from Brixton to Farringdon; it is a bit of a dog-leg journey, but I make it.

The classroom is downstairs and it's a bit gloomy, the walls are made of dark wood, compartments holding books everywhere. The five teachers are light-hearted, and not patronising; they are sincere and welcome me.

My teacher, Kate, had a slight stroke herself five years ago.

Some of the people are almost without speech; one in particular who is about twenty-five has lost the ability completely because of a stroke, and her mother comes with her to give her support. For the first time I think I have been lucky!

We are split up in to four groups; I am in the top group. There is a solicitor, a salesman, a porter, and the two girls, Lydia and I, and soon we have a friendship, though I don't have much in common with the men so much, except we have had the stroke, and everybody with a stroke is different.

We learn breathing exercises, and we sit up straight.

Kate is saying in a sing-songy voice, "Good morning." We say it back to her, "Good morning," in sing-songy voices; we are laughing!

Linda comes from north of the river; she had an embolism a year before I had a stroke. Now there is nothing wrong⊠with her physically, I don't think, just her speech. That's enough by itself.

She has a ground floor flat in Swallow Avenue, north of the river. Every now and again she has parties, or she invites me to go for a meal and Scrabble.

We take our break at one o'clock and start again at two, unless there is an outing, or when anybody has a birthday, and there is a meal at either a Chinese or Indian restaurant nearby, and it's always fun!

In addition, if a person had a stroke, and does not mix after the stroke, like me, I am very nervous, so, it's lovely socialising together, before you get to the real world as such.

One time we go on a boat trip up the River Thames, starting at Hampton Court.

All of us from Farringdon pile on the boat; some are capable of going on board with no help, others want help. Independently, I try to get myself on board with a little help from Mark, who has decided to come. I sit down because I find it rocky until they are all on board.

There is a gentle breeze as the boat takes off to the middle of the Thames. The captain doesn't need the engine at the moment, because the tide is going with the boat. Mark and I stand up at the prow of the boat looking forward, with the sun deciding to come out to join us. People are waving on the land, and me and my classmates wave back.

We settle down; nobody is talking, we are just listening to the boat as it moving along, encouraged by a warm wind and the sun. I stare at the river and touch the water with my right hand, gazing towards the land as it drifts by.

We come to a pub set back from the river with a big lawn

and tables and chairs outside. Captain Chris ties up the vessel and everybody gets off the boat. He takes the orders for drinks and lunch, and Mark offers to help, as do the partners of the other stroke survivors.

I am in my element, having my lunch and a glass of wine, surrounded by people smiling and laughing. The children are running round and round the tables, until the adults stop them, and swans and ducks eye the bread or anything the people don't want.

When I have finished my delicious lunch, I lie down on the grass, turning to face the sun, and close my eyes until it is almost time to go.

Three hours later we are back in Hampton Court. "Thank you for a great day," we chorus to Captain Chris, smiling and shaking his hand.

I feel part of the group, not apart from it. Until Farrington College, I had the feeling that I was not of this world, after my stroke; I was like another being from another planet. But after this boat ride, I feel I am gradually coming down to earth and all that comes with me being at Farringdon College.

I stay there for a whole year, which helps me enormously.

Chapter 22:

Life Goes On

After a year of speech therapy at Farringdon College, my speech gets better and better but it still isn't the same as before; if I'm nervous it comes out in my voice.

I decide to join a gospel choir at Borough College, once a week, which I find helps enormously with my speech. We do a few concerts, one at the Tate Gallery, and two at Southwark College, with practices in between once a week.

Another class is pottery, and the first thing I create is a vase, and I am surprised when it comes out of the kiln; I gaze at the blue jug with flecks on it, and I'm pleased.

The pottery teacher is pleased as well. "That's lovely, really good." He smiles at my one triumph (I have still got my blue jar, with roses in it).

I also make a large bowl - both were satisfying and pleasing to make. The wheel is something to behold, and it takes a lot of practice and working it with one and half hands is difficult.

***

Meanwhile, Mark moves upstairs into what he has made into a bedsitting room. That means he can do what he likes, which he did anyway.

We want to get some cats. "That way you won't be so lonely."

We go to Battersea Cats and Dogs Home. We think two is enough, a lovely silver tabby and his daughter, who is a beautiful tortoiseshell, with grey bits here and there in her fur. Both are adorable but just as Mark is paying the kennel girl, I can see an enormous tabby named Arthur, with a white bib and small white socks. He doesn't want to be seen, however, I see him, and ask the kennel girl about him.

Apparently, Arthur is a sad case. "We don't know how old he is, we think he is about eight or nine, maybe even older."

"I think we'll have him as well."

So, we arrive at Crystal Palace with three cats.

The silver tabby I call Dad, and his daughter, Sweetie, and they settle down immediately.

Arthur takes a bit longer; for a week he hides in the back room. He won't come out for a long time, until he comes out for food.

After a fortnight, it is bearable for him to have us around; in two months I can go up to him, he sniffs my fingers and he looks into my eyes. I stroke him, he purrs loudly; clearly, it's alright in his world now he can relax.

**

On Tom's eighteenth birthday I take the train down to Brighton and Matt picks me up from the railway station. Me and my ex-husband embrace like old friends, and he doesn't flinch when I speak. This is the first time he has seen me since my stroke.

Before we go to the house where Tom and Matt are staying, Matt takes me to a high place just outside Brighton so we can talk.

Looking out over the sea, he speaks to me with empathy. "You had a shock, didn't you? What caused it?"

"Stre-ss, I me-an do...ing to...o mu...ch, and I sup...pose smo...king and drinking to mu...ch."

Matt nods. "Yes, Mark told me a week after you had your stroke; I wanted to come to the hospital, I don't know why I didn't. Tom was upset by seeing you, obviously, I should been there with him, and supported him. But I can see that you're okay now, you're on the road to recovery, I can see that,"

We carry on talking for a while; I ask what he is doing with his band, and we chat about the old times.

Matt says, "It's good to see you. I didn't know what to expect, but you're doing well."

"As I said to my mother, I'll b-eat my str-oke in six mo-nths, she ca-me in-to the hos-pital two we-eks af-ter my str-oke, no-w i-t's thr-ee y-ears, you kn-ow? B-ut, yo-u mu-st ha-ve a se-nse of hum-our." I am laughing.

Matt looks at me and laughs with me. "I think we should get to Tom's party, don't you?"

***

Five months later, Tom comes to see me at Crystal Palace Lane; it is good to see him.

In the morning we go to Dulwich Park, because I am determined to ride my bike again, and the stroke will not defeat me.

At the park, I put my right foot on the pedal, and my left foot on the ground, and one, two and three, and up behind onto the saddle.

My steering is all over the place, I have to stop. However, I start again and the same thing happens, over and over and over. Tom is getting cold, so he runs on the spot, anything to keep him warm; it's a very cold day.

Suddenly though, after about half an hour, I master the bike. There is nothing wrong with my balance and I am able to pedal all the way round the edge of Dulwich Park. I slow down and I got off my bike near Tom.

Tom claps and I hug and kiss him. "I kn-ew I co-uld do it," I say excitedly. "Th-ank y-ou for hel-ping me." My eyes fill with tears of happiness.

Hand on heart, Tom replies, "Yes, but can we go home, please, I'm starving."

***

Tom goes off to university to study a degree in European studies. He is 23 years old, when he finishes.

I am very proud of him, particularly at his graduation.

***

After graduation, Tom gets a job in Vauxhall and comes to live with me for a year. I love having him to stay. He has many friends, and one, Philip, comes to stay overnight.

Tom asks me if I would like to go with them to a pub in Herne Hill and have something to eat afterwards.

I am delighted. "Ar-e you su-re, you don't w-ant your moth-er hang-ing arou-nd, do you?"

"Get your coat on, it's cold outside, and it's raining."

On the way, the wind and rain get worse. We're on the pavement under the bridge as the thirty-seven bus comes towards us.

It is practically dark under the bridge as the bus nearly topples in the dip in the road. The driver puts his foot down to get the bus out of the hole, just as we are parallel with him.

The bus makes an awful noise as the driver changes gear, and suddenly the bus is upon us, and a two-foot wave of water rushes over me. I am drenched, as if I have had ten buckets of water at one time thrown over me. It has missed the boys by inches.

I stand there for a moment, then turn my head and look at the bus, which is speeding away, turning right, the brakes screaming at the next stop, Herne Hill.

Tom is staring at me, trying not to laugh, and Phil is turning away. Fortunately, I can see the funny side of it, and all three of us laugh, until we reach the pub.

***

One beautiful summer's day, Tom says, "I want to take you to the Ritz, for afternoon tea, today."

"That's good of you, thank you, I think I would like that very much."

We take the train to Victoria, then the underground to Green Park, and cross over Piccadilly. Then we take a quick look at the back streets, Brick Street, Mexico Street, Shepherd Street and White Horses Way, with their low black doors and tiny windows; inside are very expensive tailors where Tom looks at the shirts and ties.

We cross the road to Piccadilly and go into the Ritz Hotel, into a sumptuous and very grand high room, called Palm Court. I look up, and see a beautiful gold trellis chandelier with elaborate metal flowers, and in the centre of the room is a large wonderful floral display.

Tom and I look at the tea menu and order. The food arrives soon after - tiny oblong white and brown sandwiches, with cheddar cheese with chutney and egg mayonnaise with shallots on the bottom plate, while on the upper plate are various cakes, a silver tea pot, cups and saucers, and small plates, that match the larger plates.

"Tha-t is beaut-iful, thank-you fo-r ta-king me." I beam at Tom.

He replies, "You're welcome. Tuck in!"

***

Tom is thinking of going to Australia with an old friend who he has known for twenty years. They visit Sydney, but after three months, they get homesick and so come home.

Back in Brighton, Tom decides to go back to university to take a master's degree, in Contemporary European studies for a year. He passes with flying colours. Obviously, again, I am very proud of him.

Chapter 23:

Twenty-Four Bridges

After five years and a lot of training, in April 1996 I'm due to take part in the Stroke Association bike ride. Along with hundreds of other people I'm going to cycle across twenty-four bridges from Tower Bridge to Hampton Court. I had my stroke in April 1986, so it's very poignant for me.

Everybody says it is ambitious, but whatever my friends think, negative and positive, I am determined to do it. I remember what Roger Wells said about my progress. It is up to me. You got one thing right, Roger!

***

My bike is stripped down, even to the basket and the mudguard; anything that is heavy has to go, and when the work is finished at the bike shop, I can virtually hold the bike up with one hand.

I decide to train in two parks, Brockwell and Dulwich park, one after the other, missing a day in between, until I am fit enough to ride every day. London is my oyster.

I travel over Vauxhall Bridge after passing Brixton, and carry on over Lambeth Bridge and turn left to Millbank, going over Westminster Bridge and eventually getting to Stamford Street, turning left towards Blackfriars and home, five times week.

Then, I go the opposite way towards Croydon, where I have friends, Neal and Susannah, and I call in for a cup of tea. But they are not there, so I slowly go home.

My mother lives in Cranbrook in Kent, and I get a train to Goudhurst, and cycle from Goudhurst to Cranbrook and back again, which is ten miles.

On another occasion I get off in Guildford, where I was

91

born, and meet up with my half-brother Jack; he is twenty-five years younger than me. Together we pedal to Cranleigh, eleven miles from Guildford, and we call in to where our father lives with Cathy, Jack's mother.

The following day, Jack and I ride around the wide rim of Cranleigh. It is a delightful ride, not particularly warm but the sun is shining and there are daffodils and crocuses down the lanes. We get off outside the pub, 'The Sun'. Jack goes inside the pub for the drinks and crisps. We talk for half an hour and then cycle back to Jack's.

I stay another night and ride back early the next morning. It is a leafy start, going northwest into Guildford and skirting the Surrey Hills, a beautiful part of the country.

I stop at Shalford, where I grew up.

I rest against the oak tree at the side of the house, remembering so many things, like the palomino pony, and my mother had so many dogs, Alsatians, whippets and puppies, a Saluki, daft but beautiful, and borders. I had English rabbits, one budgie, even a few mice and a cat as well.

I can see my father now, rushing in and out. Although, they are mainly good memories, some are bad, but fortunately not too unpleasant. I forget about them; it was a long time ago.

I munch my chocolate and a have drink before starting off again.

***

The day of the Stroke Association bike ride, the weather is beautiful. Hundreds of cyclists line up ready to go at ten o'clock on the dot. The start is at Tower Hill, then we turn west, down the hill to Monument and Mansion House.

I am getting into the rhythm and settling down to my pedalling. Blackfriars Bridge, Embankment, Southwark, Westminster and Waterloo Bridges go by. Fortunately, there are people who are glad to assist me up and down the steps if necessary. I go further on to Vauxhall Bridge and Chelsea Park where I have a break.

Then, I ride on to Putney and Barnes Bridge, where I meet Mark, who is helping me along the long wooden bridge over the Thames. I walk up on to the bridge, shaking every step of the way because I don't like heights. On the bridge, I stand there for a minute, peering through the wide planks and the long way down to the moving river.

Mark giggles. "Come on, you have to do it, don't you?" I glance at him. His arms are folded, and he is watching me; he knows that my fear is heights.

However, I know he's right, and, trembling, I move forward very slowly, holding on to the parapet with my left hand, until I reach the other side, then there are steps down on to the road. I am shaking, but I can breathe again. I thank Mark, and ride off again towards Hampton Park.

He cries, "Next time I see you, it will be Hampton Court."

"See you there."

About two-thirds of the way round, I stop at Kew Gardens for a rest again. I eat my sandwiches and a banana and have a sugary drink for energy. More people arrive with bikes - they have the same idea.

Nobody speaks, they're just smiling or nodding; it's silent apart from the noise of cans or screw top bottles, and paper.

These days, I've learned to listen to my body, so I'm aware it might seize up if I stay any longer. I'm tired, but I know that I will make it to Hampton Court. The last few miles might be the worst.

There is nobody to escort me over another smaller wooden bridge, so I have to lift the bike myself, but the wind is blowing the back of me to Hampton Court, as I climb the steps.

"Come on, come on!" I shout to myself, and, finally, I reach the top of the bridge and pedal over it, and down. 'Not far now.' That spurs me on to the road.

I have travelled the twenty-four bridges in six hours.

Mark and Jenny are at the finishing line. I am exhausted and elated as I collect my medal in the grounds of Hampton Court, my face beaming.

What is more, I have raised almost two hundred pounds in sponsorship for the Stroke Association; the four hundred participants raised around £20,000.

Chapter 24:

Different Strokes

Different Strokes is a group of stroke survivors started by an Irishman called Dondal O'Kelly, who had a stroke himself at the age of forty-five; he opened up Different Strokes in the 1990s. Dondal was a barrister until he had a stroke.

We meet in a gym on Tottenham Court Road. The group's name doesn't imply that they are necessarily different from other people; each stroke survivor has a unique experience and faces different results, whether those are major or minor.

The members are aged from eighteen to sixty. One person might look okay but can't speak, another is in a wheelchair and can talk normally. There are some really sad sights, most of whom are under sixty.

One man, Robert, had his bad stroke at the age of nine, whilst another, a pretty girl, at eighteen. So, I'm thinking once again that I have been relatively lucky.

However, a stroke can be very cruel, whatever age we might be.

There is a nurse who is a fitness instructor and she is vital in giving her time to get people moving again, once a month, whatever age they are or however damaged they are.

There is a social side to the group as well; after our meetings we go to the pub or out for a meal, and I love being in the group, it means so much to me. We are all different, but we have simply all had strokes.

Dondal O'Kelly has heard about my ride from Tower Hill to Hampton Court and he asks if I would do the Croydon to Brighton ride in July 1997. I agree, as long as others are going too.

In the end six of us go, Steve and his girlfriend Julia, who works for Different Strokes; Oliver and David, even though

David has not trained for this event and has a heavy Dutch bike; Phoebe, a sweet girl who is staying with me for a short while, she is tall, very attractive, however, she does not know it.

It is a beautiful summer's day, just right for cycling, not too warm and with no wind, only the sun playing above the branches of the trees. We meet up on the platform at Herne Hill station with our bikes.

Steve reads the map and decides on the shortest route with the tiniest roads possible.

"Okay, the first is over the North Downs!"

The train comes in and we get out at Croydon, and go quickly through the barrier and are off on the first of leg of our journey.

An hour later, we encounter the first hill of the North Downs, and nobody cycles up it, not even Steve who is quite fit. At the top of the downs, we gaze south over pockets of villages near and far, almost as far as Brighton itself, though that is not yet visible, nor is the sea.

***

We come down off the Downs and head south on a tiny road for about ten miles, until Steve slows down and then stops. He is skimming the map again, and points to a dense wood.

"Right, we have to go through here, that's the way, it's directly towards Brighton. Also, it cuts a huge chunk off the road." He is smiling at all of us, and climbs the gate with his bicycle, and we follow him, with our bikes as well.

It is colder in the woods, because the trees are tightly packed together and the sunlight has to fight to get through. It is almost spooky, because you can't hear anything, nothing at all, apart from bump, bump, bump, until we come to almost the end of the wood, and we can see sharp sunlight suddenly coming through the trees.

We stop to get our breaths back, then we clamber over another gate with our bikes again. I notice a sign saying

'PRIVATE' as we leave the wood behind and cycle down another small road.

We continue going south, up and down the hilly road, up and down, up and down; we're skirting Horsham. Five miles past the town we stop to buy an ice cream and some water in a village shop, and we eat our sandwiches in silence.

Half an hour later we reach the bottom of Ditchling Beacon, and we look at the mountainous climb. "Right," says Steve, getting the map out again. "We could go over Ditchling Beacon or around it, but going around will take us longer." He looks at us, waiting.

We look at each other and consider the feat ahead of us. We are really tired, mentally and physically, nevertheless, we look at Steve, and all declare, "Over."

My legs are weary and exhausted, as are everybody else's, and the hill is so high, it seems almost a mountain, although, without another word we start off. Many cars toot toot as we climb the Ditching Beacon, and it takes us three-quarters of an hour to reach the top.

Then we spend almost half-an-hour walking around and gazing at the beautiful scenery to help our exhaustion. It lifts us, and we lay the bikes on the ground, and we hug each other. "We've very nearly done it anyway," somebody says.

Slowly we walk to the wire fence and beyond there is a field. The air is completely silent, only broken by the cows and sheep munching grass; they don't look at us. There's a blackbird on the ground looking for worms, seemingly, he doesn't mind us either. We can hear the skylark; it sounds so sweet.

Between the meadows we can see one or two roads, much further down and the flickering windows of vans and cars, with virtually no noise except for the changing of gears and the toot, toot of the cars and lorries.

After a while, Steve says; "Shall we go?" He looks at his watch and adds, "It will be eight before we get to the pier." We are very tired, but we face no pedalling, as it is downhill, as the sun is tipping its way towards the sea, a superb and stunning sight welcoming us as we go into Brighton.

It's almost dark when we ride into town. Robert meets us at the seafront by the pier.

"Well done," he says, kissing the girls, and shaking hands with the men.

"There's a curry house around the corner over there," Robert says enthusiastically; he is pointing to George Street, on the left side. So, we pick up our bicycles and very slowly head off to the Indian restaurant. We are very are hungry and we pile into the restaurant. We devour our meal with not much talking at all as we are all so desperately weary. Only Robert keeps the conversation going.

After an hour and a half, we come out of the curry house and we walk slowly up to Brighton station for a train to London and home.

Chapter 25:

I Wonder

I wonder sometimes how different my life would have been if I hadn't had the stroke and my speech was normal. I remember how I used to speak and how my voice sounded, however, that was a long time ago, and sometimes, particularly when I am tired, I will lose the meaning half way through a sentence, and maybe someone will finish it for me.

But, when I am angry, my voice is almost crystal clear.

So many people have avoided me over the years, who probably wouldn't have if I had not had the stroke. Every day I think about my stroke, some way or another.

My good sense of humour keeps me going. I enjoy laughter, and sometimes I wonder whether people are laughing with me or at me? I am finding few genuine friendships and my true friends in particular, will always laugh with me, and do. Simon is such a friend, who I met in London just before 2000, in October 1999.

Also, I am more determined to face whatever life is throwing at me. Being an only child, I was always alone, and children didn't flock to me, so this sense of aloneness has continued to be with me into adulthood.

The day of the stroke was devastating for me and others around me, and it has only strengthened my feelings of isolation and solitude.

Simon did not know me before the stroke, so it's easy for him, in some ways, and my lovely daughter-in-law and my grandchildren see me as Emma or Grandma Emma. Tom sees it totally differently, and understandably, he knew me before the stroke; it's so different for him, we never talk about it.

I quite like being alone, especially if I have something to do.

So now, having spent almost half my life with a stroke, I am learning to live with it, not always willingly. For example, since my stroke I still limp, but it is getting better and my right hand sometimes feels better and on other days it doesn't want to know.

More challenging are people! I am good in a one to one, or if I know the people in small groups. But I am not good at large crowds, I get swamped and overwhelmed, and I say silly things to people, maybe not all the time, but sometimes I wish the ground would swallow me up.

The worse side effect of the stroke is people being patronising to me, that is the worst thing of all. But if they could just calm down and treat me as they do everyone else, see me and not the stroke, then that would be fine.

I sometimes have awkward moments when someone doesn't know me, and they look at me as if I am making a hash of it, and so I will make hash of it!

But this is going to be as good as it is gets, and I have come triumphantly through it. I am grateful for that.

A good friend of mine asked me why I wrote the story in the first place.

It's for lots of reasons. I like writing and words. It's a wonderful thing to do as well and I think I have a tale to tell.

***

I moved to Littlehampton in 2004, and Mark moved back into the house we shared. Unfortunately, he died in 2006. He had cancer - he knew but he didn't do anything about it. Regrettably, I didn't know either, until he passed away. Until then, he was one of the people I could call upon. Part of me will always love him.

***

On a beautiful summer's day, in the kitchen of the house in Littlehampton, which is now exactly the way I want it, out in the back garden, I see a blackbird flying.

EPILOGUE

I met Professor Nick Ward briefly twice; at the World Stroke Association Forum in Victoria, London, then again at U.C.L Queen's Square at the Institute of Neurology for Upper Limb Rehabilitation recovery.

He and a therapist looked at my arm and hand thoroughly. They came to the conclusion that I take a three weeks intensive course in 2020 - the Upper Limb Programme. My arm hadn't been looked at for thirty-four years, since April 1986. I was delighted and jumped at the chance of being almost whole again.

The first stage was to meet the team, which included an occupational therapist, a physiotherapist and a rehabilitation assistant. They quickly worked out what I was able to do with my arm and hand, which was not a lot it seemed, but the therapists were encouraging.

My excuse is that I have always had a dominant left hand. However, therapists don't give up, even after thirty-four years, the goal was to make me whole again in my right arm and particularly the right hand. They gave me various exercises, for example, doing up buttons on a blouse, holding pots and pans in my right hand, and many others. When I left there, finally, I was given independent exercises when I went home.

All I can say is, it is working for my arm and particularly my hand, very slowly. I can see it is working, and if I can keep it up for three, six, seven months or however long it takes, it is up to me. I think, it is your will, that is the key. Furthermore, the therapists, they want to see that it works as well.

Thank you so very much, Professor Nick Ward and the lovely therapists and all who were involved in the U.C.L. Upper Limb Programme – thank you so much for the opportunity to make my arm right again.

Printed in Great Britain
by Amazon

52720411R00069